Cultural diversity in the arts

Art, art policies and
the facelift of Europe

edited by
Ria Lavrijsen

Royal Tropical Institute – The Netherlands

Cultural diversity in the arts was published with financial support from the Dutch Ministry of Welfare, Health and Cultural Affairs, the Amsterdam City Council, the European Cultural Foundation, the British Council, the Arts Council of Great Britain, Maison Descartes, the Goethe Institut and UNESCO (World Decade for Cultural Development), which also supported the seminar «Cultural diversity in the arts» at the Soeterijn / Royal Tropical Institute, February 1993.

The book is published as a pendant to *Art, anthropology and the modes of re-presentation,* edited by Harry Leyten en Bibi Damen and with contributions by Frits Bless, David Elliott, Paul Faber, Frans Fontaine, Fieke Konijn, Harrie Leyten, Sebastiàn López.

Royal Tropical Institute
Soeterijn
63 Mauritskade
1092 AD Amsterdam
The Netherlands
020-5688711

Photograph front cover: «Like a bird» by Iléne Themen (1988)

Contents

Preface

On February 9 and 10, 1993, an international conference on «Cultural diversity in the arts» was held in Amsterdam by Soeterijn, the theatre of the Royal Tropical Institute. This conference was one of the events of the spring 1993 project «The facelift of Europe», which featured, in addition to conferences, film, dance, theatre, and the visual arts. The aim of the conference «Cultural diversity in the arts» was to generate a discussion on art and participation and representation in Europe's multicultural cities in the nineties, between artists, art critics, publicists, theorists, administrators and educators of both Western and of non-Western descent. In order to discuss cultural diversity, profound cultural and philosophical reflection is required on current art practice, policy-making, and art history. The conference provided a platform for this academic reflection and hopefully it was successful in clarifying crucial issues which crop up repeatedly in the discourse between artists, policy-makers and publicists from different cultures.

This publication reproduces the lectures, workshop reports and recommendations for future art policy in various European countries. We would especially like to thank Homi Bhabha, Rosi Braidotti, Remo Guidieri, Lola Young, and Anthony Everitt for their challenging and inspiring keynote lectures, most of which we are able to publish here, as well as Trevor Phillips, who during the conference created through his open style of presentation and his energetic chairing of the debates an atmosphere truly conducive to discussion. We also wish to express our thanks to Aad Nuis, Dutch member of parliament, who kindly opened the conference, and Tijmen van Grootheest, Director for Fine Arts, Architecture and Design of the Dutch Ministry of Welfare, Health and Cultural Affairs, who demonstrated the government's concern with the subject of the conference in receiving its recommendations. Special thanks also go to Helen Denniston, Tony van Dijk and Gavin Jantjes whose papers were a great inspiration to the workshop discussions, and Ton Bevers, Rik van Hulst, and John Stringham who were kind enough to make time to chair the workshop sessions.

We also wish to thank Mr A. Apostolou, Eltje Bos, David Pinto, Hortence Sarmaat, Cas Smithuijsen, Ernst Veen, and Walter Palm, members of the advisory board of «Cultural diversity in the arts», and Marjan Schweitzer, Pierre Ballings and Bram Buijze for their excellent advice and support. We are

7

indebted to all the artists, cultural philosophers, policy-makers and publicists from the different European countries who attended the workshops and contributed so enthusiastically and constructively to the debates.

We greatly acknowledge the support of the Dutch Ministry of Welfare, Health and Cultural Affairs, the Amsterdam City Council, the European Cultural Foundation, the British Council, the Arts Council of Great Britain, Maison Descartes, the Goethe-Institut and UNESCO (World Decade for Cultural Development), and appreciate the confidence they expressed in us.

And last but not least, we would like to thank all those all over Europe, from the most diverse backgrounds, who took the time to inform us about books, articles, and reports available on these issues, and were helpful to us in so many other ways during our research.

Ria Lavrijsen
Otto Romijn, Soeterijn

Introduction

Today many people of Asian, Arab, African, or Afro-Caribbean descent have settled in Europe's large cities, in London, Birmingham, Paris, Berlin, Brussels, Amsterdam, Rotterdam and The Hague. This has engendered forms of transcultural communication in these metropoles, as people of different cultures seek to understand and respect each other. It also means – as lecturer and publicist Homi Bhabha points out – that Europe can no longer count on the comfort and continuities of tradition. 'Where once we could believe in the comfort and continuities of tradition, today we must face the responsibilities of cultural translation. In the attempts to mediate between different cultures, languages and societies, there is always the threat of mistranslation, confusion and fear.' (Bhabha, 1989, p. 12)

In Europe three attitudes towards non-Western cultures can be discriminated: the relativist attitude, the universalist attitude, and the pluralist attitude. Neither the relativist attitude, whereby Europeans of Western and non-Western descent do not judge each other's values and norms, nor the universalist attitude, whereby Western values are regarded as universal, have proved effective or fruitful for transcultural communication. As a result, we face the challenging task of developing new pluralist values and norms. The recent demographic shifts are expected to produce changes in art production and give rise to new audiences in the large European cities. These will to an increasing extent be multiracial and multicultural. Such cultural diversity raises issues of mounting urgency for art institutions and art schools in countries throughout Europe, including the Netherlands.

In the eighties, it was predicted that by the end of 1991 migrant artists in the Netherlands would no longer be able to rely on specific budgets. At present, the government's subsidy policies are aimed at integration and all artists seeking a grant are subject to the same assessment procedures, irrespective of their cultural background. These government policies pre-suppose that art institutions and art schools are capable of developing new creative and innovative policies and syllabuses to cater for culturally diverse arts and artists who, with or without a personal bond with non-Western cultures, now form part of the European culture and present art scene.

Cultural identity

Art institutions in Europe in the nineties will find themselves faced with a growing number of artists and students using styles and expressions such as fusion, hybridisation, and syncretism which are no longer either purely Western or non-Western. A dialogue between art institutions and art practitioners from culturally diverse backgrounds is an essential step towards integration. No art institution can afford to shelve the problem of cultural diversity. Arbiters involved in the assessment of art in the nineties, whether they be of European, Asian, Arab, African, or Afro-Caribbean descent, will have to ask themselves whether they are equipped to judge culturally diverse art.

At this moment, the problem of cultural identity is a major issue in many European countries. On the one hand, we observe the emergence of a global culture, aided by mass media and technology, which have intensified the communication between cultures, peoples and nations throughout the world. On the other hand, however, we discern an increasing fragmentation into nationalist movements and ethnocentrism between separate ethnic communities and other factions of society. While national governments are worried about the national cultural identity, many artists of both Western and non-Western descent are profoundly concerned with their personal, and artistic cultural identity. Some artists with a non-European background regard themselves in the first place as, for instance, Black or Turkish, while others wishing to broaden the notion of identity, see themselves as artists who happen to be both Black and British or Dutch or happen to be of Turkish descent. According to Nikos Papastergiadis, publicist and editor of *Third Text*, it is important 'to see the migrant artist's work not just as a representation of the place of origin and the place of arrival, but also as a metaphor for the processes of journeying.' (Papastergiadis, 1991, p. 46)

We must address the question of what kind of support and limitations artists of culturally diverse backgrounds experience when working within White and European art institutions. At the same time, however, we must ask what kind of support and constraints artists experience within their own communities. How critical are artists of culturally diverse backgrounds allowed to be by their own ethnic communities or the European art world of which they now form a part?

Spaces in-between

Homi Bhabha, one of the prominent speakers at the conference, discusses in chapter 1 the issue of cultural identity and the relationship between the centre and the periphery, dealing with the notions 'beyond' and 'interstices', i.e., the 'spaces in-between'. Bhabha is particularly concerned with what takes place *beyond* the centre. Cultural identity, according to Bhabha, cannot be defined in terms of race, ethnicity or nationality. The late twentieth century has witnessed the emergence of a complexity of cultural identities, which are further complicated by such crucial factors as gender and class, as well as the tension between tradition and modernity. Factors such as race, ethnicity, nationality, class, gender, sexual and religious orientation, tradition and modernism all shade that identity. Sometimes these elements fuse harmoniously, but more often they clash. According to Bhabha, these elements are constantly in negotiation and competition with one another. As well as possibly creating tension between groups of people, there may be tension between these elements within one and the same person.

The system of ideological 'pillarisation' applied in the Netherlands is often considered successful. Under this system, every religious and ethnic group is allowed to develop within its own community, fostering a peaceful coexistence within the community as a whole. But one may question whether this segregated system is fruitful for the arts. Whereas religious sectarianism may be defensible, a separatism based on ethnicity, descent or race can be contested. A fixed and essentialised cultural identity on the basis of race or origin is bound to conflict with the dynamic nature of art, for art is essentially a history of broken identities.

Homi Bhabha believes that what goes on in the transitional areas between the cultural communities is of crucial significance to the arts. He calls these spaces in between 'interstices'. It is in these boundary areas that exciting developments are taking place and that fundamental renewal in the arts can be expected. Similarly, Stuart Hall advocates abandoning the idea of a fixed or essentialised Black cultural identity by giving undivided creative attention not to the homogeneity of Black experience but to the diversity. (Stuart Hall, 1992)

Rosi Braidotti, whose publication *Patterns of dissonance* (1991) constituted an important contribution to the debate on the relationship between feminism, philosophy and culture, discusses in chapter 2 her notion of 'nomads in a transformed Europe'. 'Nomad' is used to designate people who move from

11

place to place. Braidotti, however, uses the word as a metaphor for a specific way of life, for people who are at home everywhere and nowhere, and who are not readily classified in fixed nationalistic, ethnic or gender-based categories. She sees nomadism as a new state of consciousness which could bring about a transformation in Europe in the years to come.

Lola Young seeks in chapter 3 to identify potential for alliances to be made in the shared sense of alienation and fragmentation which characterises postmodern existence for many people. Further, she examines the way in which artists and intellectuals of Afro-Caribbean and Indian descent constituted crucial interventions in the debate about identity and how the British arts sector has responded to these interventions in recent decades through a policy of multiculturalism. Lola Young pleads for a policy that eliminates all discriminatory procedures instead of a multiculturalism as a salve to guilty consciences.

Anthony Everitt, Secretary General of the Arts Council of Great Britain, reflects in his contribution entitled 'The Emperor's spectacles' on the disadvantages of a top-down policy of multiculturalism and questions whether the former relativism of interculturalism did not offer a better perspective. He favours a heterogeneous art policy which would give prominence to a new form of internationalism.

Quality or qualities?

The second part of this publication addresses, among others – like the conference – the problem of defining quality in the arts. Non-Western and culturally diverse contributions to modern and contemporary art have often been ignored by art historians. One explanation might be that European-based artists with mixed experience from non-Western and Western cultures introduce new aesthetics and an assortment of hybrid art forms. Homi Bhabha advocates rethinking the language of a community as a cultural unity from a post-colonial viewpoint in order to allow for diversified cultural and political boundaries, and a hybridisation of cultural influence. 'The crucial question is whether the universalism, that is often inherent in the expansive, empathetic impulse to "simultaneously translate" cultures, can provide us with the critical space appropriate to the contradictory and hybrid cultural identities that distinguish the histories of nations towards the end of our century.' (Bhabha, 1990)

If parameters such as originality, dramatic impact, eloquence, expressivity, imagination, aestheticism, craftsmanship, professionalism, inspiration, and richness of ideas are used when judging art, one should take into account that these words may have different meanings not only in different cultures but also for different people within one ethnic community. According to Homi Bhabha, 'we cannot place ourselves in that Archimedean space of neutrality between "world cultures", in a kind of *musée imaginaire;* nor can we espouse the nativist perspective that speaks assertively, on the basis of its own "authentic", pure cultural particularism.' (Bhabha, 1990)

The American art critic Lucy R. Lippard writes that the conventional notion of good taste with which many people were raised and educated was based on an illusion of social order that is no longer possible or desirable to believe in. 'We now look at art within the context of disorder – a far more difficult task than following institutionalized regulations.' (Lippard, 1990) Supporters of this conventional notion of good taste very often think in the dichotomies of Western/non-Western, superior/inferior, modern/traditional, centre/periphery, and high art/low art. It is interesting to consider whether it is possible to abandon this divisive either/or attitude in favour of a compromise between the political radicalism of 'deconstructivists' and 'political correctness' on the one hand, and the conventional liberalism of the Western art world, which pretends to recognise universal quality in art, on the other.

The question is whether in the nineties leeway will be granted for new and other visions of quality, voiced by people who are not part of established art circles. These groups are eager to participate in the art world, as arbiters who stand open to other qualities, to cultural differences, to other aesthetics and other parameters, to a renewal of modern and postmodern art, and to a recognition of pluralism.

New connections

The second topic discussed here concerns participation, and, in particular, programming, audience development and education. «New connections: Finding tomorrow's audience today», the title of the fifth annual congress of the International Society of Performing Arts Administrators (ISPAA), held in June 1991, made a perfect title for this conference theme. Large culturally diverse populations have settled not only in American cities such as Los

Angeles, New York and Chicago but also in the European cities of Paris, Berlin, London, and Amsterdam. These big European cities are populated by new Europeans of every conceivable background: first, second and third generation citizens of Asian, Arab, African, and Afro-Caribbean descent, as well as people with mixed backgrounds. In a city like Amsterdam, 25 per cent of the population has some connection with a non-Western culture. In Amsterdam almost 50 per cent of the primary school children aged between six and twelve has a culturally diverse background.

In the nineties, art schools and art institutions will have to cater for a growing number of students and artists from culturally diverse backgrounds, and audiences will become increasingly multicultural and multiracial. By relating population figures in Europe to factors such as birth-rate, migration and mortality, demographers have made predictions about the population in the year 2000. As for the Netherlands, it is predicted that in the year 2032 between nine and seventeen per cent of the population may be from a culturally diverse background. (WRR, 1989) For some European countries, these figures might be even higher. How do city-planners, policy makers and arts administrators plan to accommodate these changes? Michel Giraud, chairman of the 1990 Melbourne conference «Metropolis», says: 'From now on, urban planning and humanism are indissociable and beyond urban projects and policies for large installations, we must seek social cohesions and refuse exclusions.' (Les Cahiers no. 9, 1991) If these words are not just fashionable rhetoric, city-planners and policy makers cannot only consider arts in terms of economic growth, box office revenue and international prestige. They will have to look very carefully at the changes already taking place in European cities and the changes envisaged in the near future.

Dr August Coppola, Dean of the School of Creative Arts, San Francisco State University, remarked at the above-mentioned «New Connections» conference: 'While demographic statistics merely tell us how many others are out there, we have a need to understand who those others are.' One way to discover this is to have what Coppola calls 'metaphoric detachment', meaning some insight into life, into the imagination, into feelings by which we can group our thoughts in various ways. 'The key, then, is not how many African Americans or Latinos or Asians there are in this country, but rather what these cultures represent. If we could feel the "tickle" of other cultures, we might begin to be able to really communicate with one another.' (New connections, 1991, p. 12)

The challenge in the nineties for arts administrators, policy makers, and

14

artists throughout Europe will be to find ways of deep understanding to cross national, cultural and ethnic boundaries. Cultural critic Kobena Mercer stresses: '... we need to move towards an analysis of the contradictory identifications of which we are politically capable. This means turning the search for roots – the desire for a fixed centre of identity – into a search for routes out of the prisonhouse of marginality, to which the hierarchical ordering of difference would have us consigned, each in our own little ideological bantustan.' (Mercer, 1992, p. 38)

In his essay *Cultuurspreiding en publieksbereik* (1990) (Spreading culture and reaching audiences), Dutch publicist and cultural critic Ton Bevers states that participation in culture and the arts and the stimulation of participation can be achieved if there is a connection with people's frames of reference. Theatres and museums must address the problem of how to implement innovative policies. The policy of one of Europe's greatest art institutions, The South Bank Centre in London, served as a starting point for the discussions on programming, audience development and education.

Crossing boundaries

A third major theme concerns the crossing of boundaries: art policy in a multicultural society. Different art policies are deployed by different European countries. In the Netherlands, for instance, the Arts Council (made up of artists and experts) acts as an advisory body to the Ministry of Welfare, Health and Cultural Affairs, which decides how funds are allocated. Beside acting as an advisory body, the Arts Council in the United Kingdom is also responsible for allocating funds. In France, the involvement of political and governmental institutions in the allocation of funds is greater than in both the United Kingdom and the Netherlands. In Germany every federal state has its own art policy.

Three approaches may be distinguished in the discussions on cultural diversity in these countries. First, there are those who support a specific policy for ethnic groups. This policy seeks to maintain fixed cultural identities, and to conserve or cultivate the arts and culture of each specific ethnic group. The premise for such a policy is the notion that a society may be divided into ethnic segments whose cultures should be represented on the national and European art scene. Cultural difference is here defined in terms of racial and ethnic characteristics. Therefore such a specific policy based on ethnic chauvinism would ultimately result in segregation or apartheid, as some people say.

A second approach favours policies aimed at assimilation. This view asserts that people from different cultures and races should adjust to the dominant national or European cultures. Supporters of assimilation require artists to adjust to European-based definitions of quality and ways of communication in the arts and art education. But one may question whether a homogeneous national or European culture exists. Europe has always known historical, cultural and experiential differences within and between communities, nations, regions, and cities. The idea of one European homogenised culture is a myth, as is the idea of homogenised cultural identities within specific non-European ethnic groups. However, because of the power structures within the art world, and its increasing orientation to the mass media and to commercial and market demands, there is a tendency towards homogeneity in national, European and global cultures.

Opponents of both ethnic chauvinism and faceless universalism in Europe are more sympathetic towards a policy aimed at integration and pluralism. Such a policy is founded on the principle that a society is made up of individuals each with a specific historical and cultural background. Adherents of this view recognise that cultural identity is determined by a complexity of factors: ethnicity, aspects of the culture of the former mother country and the new homeland, class, sex, religious orientation, sexual orientation, aspects of rural and urban culture. They also recognise that different European countries, regions, and ethnic communities may have something in common as well as cultural differences. Such differences are non-hierarchical in a pluralist society. Not only will the dominant national and European cultures modify, but also the cultures of the ethnic communities will undergo change. Supporters of this policy will speak in terms of qualities as opposed to quality, of aesthetics rather than a single aesthetic, of histories instead of history. This vision guarantees the heterogeneity of cultures.

In her book *Mixed blessings* (1990), Lucy R. Lippard points out that the boundaries being tested today by dialogue are not just racial and national. 'They are also those of gender and class, of value and belief systems, of religion and politics. The borderlands are porous, restless, often incoherent territory, virtual minefields of unknowns for both practitioners and theoreticians. Cross-cultural, cross-class, cross-gender relations are strained.' Lippard continues: 'In the art world there remains a divisive either/or

16

attitude towards people of color, women, gays, lesbians, working people and the poor. This is often as obvious in the Marxist and social democratic rhetoric of some "deconstructionists" as it is in the less rigorous rhetoric of conventionally liberal art historians.' (Lippard, 1990) It is, of course, very difficult to devise a clear strategy that intermediate between the binary model that defines things in terms of oppositions – oppressor/oppressed, man/woman, Black/White, power/powerless, and good/bad – and the apolitical approach of the art world that takes no account of the specific societal context in which art is produced.

«Cultural diversity in the arts» was chosen as the title of the conference and this book in preference to the 'migrant arts' or 'minority arts' since cultural diversity embraces differences of class, culture, region, religion, and gender and allows us to examine these from a non-essentialised and open perspective. The terms 'migrant arts' and 'minority arts' are too readily associated with ethnic backgrounds and country of origin and tend to suggest the existence of a homogeneous migrant or minority culture. We believe in the capability of people of diverse backgrounds to transcend boundaries and create new, dynamic and non-essentialised cultural identities and we hope that this publication will help to heighten an awareness of the cultural diversity which hallmarks the change in arts in Europe today. A change that will prove to be more than just a cosmetic facelift.

Ria Lavrijsen

Opening address

A long time ago, at the end of the fifties, I lived in Jamaica for some years. There I met a local artist who made a lifelong impression on me. He was not, at the time, recognised as an artist by the public that decides on such things. He lived in a small, crowded room in a shanty town near Kingston, where he was the shepherd or leader of a small religious community. The religion he practised was a curious mixture of Christian and traditional African elements. He had no formal education and no training in the arts, but he was highly intelligent and his work had real force. Everything he did, his sermons and his magic, his storytelling, woodcarving and painting, his endless questioning of casual visitors, served one purpose only: forming a comprehensive view of life out of all the odds and ends he could lay his hands on, old and new. He was building a shanty of the mind, a habitable shelter in a world that seemed to make no sense, for himself and the people who asked for his guidance.

Culture, as the way to make sense of life: it is an abstract proposition that is valid everywhere. But never before had I seen the raw urgency of that search so clearly as in that grim environment of poverty and loss of traditions, loss of community, direction, of hope. And never after have I shared the condescending view that regards the cultures that arose in the shanty towns of the world, forging themselves with bare hands out of the broken remnants of traditional ways of life and the throw-offs of Western mass-culture, as 'hybrid', as somehow inferior to the authenticity of the ancestors or the purity of high Western art. Everywhere I noticed the same urgency in those new cultures, that stark necessity to make sense of life, as a matter of survival.

The culture of the centres of the West was and is no shanty at all. It was and is a huge, glittering department store, with separate floors for religion and philosophy, for the arts and sciences, for popular entertainment, for high art. The urgent need to make sense of the world is still there in the work of individual artists and writers, sometimes also in movements with a mission such as feminism, but it hardly shows in the mass of consumers that throng along the counters, pick and choose among the riches, show good taste rather than great hunger and may turn the lifeblood of an artist into the fad of one season.

Meanwhile, the hybrid cultures of the third world as well as its great unbroken cultural traditions have come to the great cities of the West, together with the people who are their carriers. They still have their particular urgency, it may even be stronger in a world that is so baffling to those who have only just come to it. But they run the risk of being sucked up by the department store and lose their vitality after a short, bright life on the novelty counters. On the other hand, if they try and keep themselves totally apart in an alien world, they will no longer really make sense of that world in which their people nonetheless have to live. For the others, the general public of the great Western department store, they would be, more than ever, cute and quaint and interesting and not to be taken serious really.

The extreme relativist attitude towards other cultures comes down to the same thing as universalist arrogance in the end: to the negation of the urgency and seriousness of other peoples' attempts to make sense of their own lives, and of our common world. Different cultures inhabit the same streets of our cities, each culture with its unique character and force. They may try to ignore each other, but they will never again succeed completely in that; they will interact and change in that interaction, the dominant culture as well as the immigrant cultures. We will have to devise ways to find and maintain unity of purpose in a wide diversity of approaches to life and art, to keep the vital warmth of the cultural quest alive in the cold glamour of the department store, to have the courage of our values and convictions, but to remain in touch.

This is the subject of the «Cultural diversity in the arts» conference in the city of Amsterdam, a city that sustained its first great wave of immigrant cultures about four centuries ago, and has never outlived the thrill of it. I express the hope that the discussions on cultural diversity in the arts, elaborated in this publication, will continue to be profound and spirited and also practical, so that humble policy makers such as I may profit from the results.

Aad Nuis

1   Beyond the pale: Art in the age of multicultural translation [*]

Homi K. Bhabha

A boundary is not that at which something stops but, as the Greeks recognised, the boundary is that from which *something begins its presencing*. Heidegger, *Building, dwelling, thinking.* (1971)

It is the trope of our times to locate the question of culture in the realm of the *beyond*. At the century's edge, we are less exercised by annihilation – the death of the author – or epiphany – the birth of the 'subject'. Our existence, today, is marked by a tenebrous sense of survival, living on the borderlines of the 'present', for which there seems to be no proper name other than that shifting prefix 'post': postmodernism, postcolonialism, postfeminism.... The 'beyond' is neither a new horizon, nor a leaving behind of the past. (...) Beginnings and endings may be the sustaining myths of the middle years; but in the *fin de siècle*, we find ourselves in the moment of transit where space and time cross to produce complex figures of difference and identity, past and present, inside and outside, inclusion and exclusion. For, above all else, there is a sense of disorientation, a disturbance of direction in the 'beyond': an exploratory, restless movement caught so well in the French rendition of the word *au delà*, here and there, on all sides, *fort/da*, hither and thither, back and forth. (Showalter, 1990, pp. 1-18)

The move away from the singularities of 'class' or 'gender' as primary conceptual and organisational categories has resulted in an awareness of the multiple subject positions – of race, gender, generation, institutional location, geopolitical locale, sexual orientation – that inhabit any claim to identity in the (post)modern world. It is in the emergence of the interstices – the overlap and displacement of domains of social difference – that the intersubjective and collective experiences of 'nationness', community interest, or cultural value

---

* I would like to thank David Joselit and Elisabeth Sussman for their extremely useful comments; and David Ross for making my task harder, and the result, I hope, better.

are negotiated. How are subjects formed 'in-between', or in excess of, the sum of the 'parts' of difference (usually intoned as race, class, gender etc.)? How do strategies of representation or empowerment come to be formulated in the competing claims of communities where, despite shared histories of deprivation and discrimination, the exchange of values, meanings and priorities may not always be collaborative and dialogical, but may be profoundly antagonistic, conflictual and even incommensurable?

The force of these questions is born out by the 'language' of recent social crises sparked off by histories of cultural difference. Conflicts in South Central Los Angeles between Koreans and African-Americans focused on the concept of 'disrespect' – a term forged on the borderlines of ethnic deprivation that is, at once, the sign of racialised violence and the symptom of the social victimage of migrants in the Western metropolis. In the aftermath of the *The satanic verses* affair in Great Britain, Black and Irish feminists, despite their different constituencies, have made common cause against the 'racialisation of religion' as the dominant discourse through which the State represents their conflicts and struggles, however secular or even 'sexual' their liberationist aims may be.

Terms of cultural engagement, whether antagonistic or affiliative, are produced performatively: 'difference' is not so much a reflection of pre-given ethnic or cultural traits set in the tablets of 'fixed' traditions as it is a complex on-going negotiation – amongst minorities, against assimilation. The 'right' to signify concerns not so much the celebration of the persistence of tradition as much as an acknowledgement of its powers of reinscription and iteration: its forms of displacement and relocation. The borderline engagements of cultural difference may as often be consensual as conflictual; they may confound our definitions of tradition and modernity; re-align the customary boundaries between the private and the public, high and low; and challenge normative expectations of development and progress.

Representing cultures 'at the borderlines' is a demanding double act between artist and curator. What ensues is not, as was once believed, the flagrant contradiction[*] between the museum as a space of containment or

---

[*]   I hope it is quite clear that my discussion on the problems of going beyond *or* outside the
       museum focuses on conceptual issues involved in 'imaging' and imagining institutions.
       I have no doubt at all that the art-market attempts to turn the exhibition into a space of
       commodification: the making of reputations, the marketability of styles and fashions.
       This is not, however, the issue I am dealing with here.

'normalisation', and radical art practices, opposed to commodification, striving to give birth to a public space without walls. There is something too schematic about this demarcation of what it means to be inside or outside an institution, or an ideology; a strident separation that loses the sense that 'museums necessarily conjoin contradictory desires, including the mature (propertied) and the youthful (less so) and perhaps even the reactionary and the subversive; (...) the nature of museumgoing emmeshes the seemingly serious and the apparently voyeuresque'.[*] (Boon, 1991, p. 260) Installed within the very act of display, in the contradictory structure of spectatorship itself, there exists an ambivalence about the representation of cultural difference, which creates a productive tension between the borderline artist and the frontline curator or critic.

The borderline artist performs a poetics of the open-border between cultures. She displays the 'interstices', the overlappings and interleavings, the hither and thither that is part of the history of those peoples whose identities are crafted from the experience of social displacement. Slaves, indentured labourers, economic minorities, political refugees, sexual or ethnic minorities must neither be homogenised into an 'ontology of the oppressed', nor celebrated as the mutinous 'margins' of the metropolitan experience. Their specificity lies in an ethics of cultural survival: their minority positions provide a tracery of the transnational world where links between cultures and communities are made through the struggle against cultural marginalisation, with the will to empowerment, rather than the vainglorious conceits of social centrality and political hegemony. Borderline artists may have fragmented narratives, archives that are empty, memories that are potent yet powerless; but their experience of survival gives them a special insight into the constructed, artefactual, strategic, and contingent nature of those events that are memorialised, by the powerful, as being the 'facts' of life, or the reportage of historical record.

'I wanted to make shapes or set up situations that are kind of open.(...) My work has a lot to do with a kind of fluidity, a movement back and forth, not making a claim to any specific or essential way of being ...' writes Renee Green, the African-American artist. She reflects on the need to understand cultural difference as the production of minority identities that 'split' – are

---

[*]   Cited in Karp and Lavine. We are all greatly indepted to Karp and Lavine for initiating a
     debate on display and cultural 'displacement', which is crucially important for any
     discussion of the politics of representation.

estranged unto themselves – in the act of being articulated into a collective body. Political empowerment, and the enlargement of the multiculturalist cause, come from posing questions of solidarity and community from the interstitial perspective. Social differences are not simply given to experience through an already authenticated cultural tradition; they are the signs of the emergence of community envisaged as a project – at once a vision and a construction – that takes you 'beyond' yourself in order to return, in a spirit of revision and reconstruction, to the political conditions of the present: 'Even then, it is still a struggle for power between various groups within ethnic groups about what's being said and who's saying what, who's representing who? What is a community anyway? What is a black community? What is a Latino community? I have trouble with thinking of all these things as monolithic fixed categories'. (Green, p. 6)

If Renee Green's questions open up an interrogatory space between the act of representation – who? what? where? – and the presence of community itself, then consider her own creative intervention within this in-between moment. Green's 'architectural' site-specific work, *Sites of genealogy* displays and displaces the binary logic through which identities of difference are often constructed – Black/White, Self/Other. Green makes, in a conversation with Donna Harkavy, curator of the Worcester Museum, a metaphor of the museum building itself, rather than simply using the gallery space: '...I used architecture literally as a reference, using the attic, the boiler room, and the stair well to make associations between certain binary divisions such as higher and lower and heaven and hell. The stairwell became a liminal space, a pathway between the upper and lower areas, each of which was annotated with plaques referring to blackness and whiteness ...'

The stairwell as liminal space, in-between the designations of identity, becomes the process of symbolic interaction, the connective tissue that constructs the difference between upper and lower, Black and White. The hither and thither of the stairwell, the temporal movement and passage that it allows, prevents identities at either end of it from settling into primordial polarities. This interstitial passage *in-between* fixed identifications opens up the possibility of a cultural hybridity that entertains difference without hierarchy: 'I always went back and forth between racial designations and designations from physics or other symbolic designations. All these things blur in some way. (...) To develop a genealogy of the way colours and noncolours function is interesting to me.'

If the jargon of our times – postmodernity, postcoloniality, postfeminism –

24

has any meaning at all, it does not lie in the popular use of the 'post' to indicate sequentiality after-feminism; or polarity – anti-modernism. These terms that insistently gesture to the beyond only embody its restless and revisionary energy if they transform the present into an expanded and ex-centric site of experience and empowerment. For instance, if the interest in postmodernism is limited to a celebration of the fragmentation of the 'grand narratives' of post-Enlightenment rationalism then, for all its intellectual excitement, it remains a profoundly Eurocentric enterprise.

The wider significance of the postmodern condition lies in the awareness that the epistemological 'limits' of those ethnocentric ideas are also the enunciative boundary of a range of other dissonant, even dissident histories and voices – women, the colonised, minority groups, the bearers of policed sexualities. For the demography of the new internationalism is the history of postcolonial migration, the narratives of cultural and political diaspora, the major social displacements of peasant and aboriginal communities, the poetics of exile, the grim prose of political and economic refugees. It is in this sense that the boundary, according to Heidegger, is the place from which something begins its presencing in a movement not dissimilar to the ambulant, ambivalent articulation of the beyond that I have drawn out: 'Always and ever differently the bridge escorts the lingering and hastening ways of men to and fro, so that they may get to other banks. (...) The bridge gathers as a passage that crosses...' (Heidegger, 1971, pp. 152-153)

The very concepts of homogenous national cultures, the concensual or contiguous transmission of historical traditions, or 'organic' ethnic communities – as the grounds of cultural comparativism – are in a profound process of redefinition. Contemporary Sri Lankan theatre represents the deadly conflict between the Tamils and the Sinhalese through allegorical references to state brutality in South Africa and Latin America; the Anglo-Celtic canon of Australian literature and cinema is being re-written from the perspective of Aboriginal political and cultural imperatives; the South African novels of Richard Rive, Bessie Head, Nadine Gordimer, John Coetzee are documents of a society divided by the effects of Apartheid that enjoin the international intellectual community to meditate on the unequal, asymmetrical worlds that exist elsewhere; Salman Rushdie writes the fabulist historiography of post-Independence India and Pakistan in *Midnight's children* and *Shame*, only to remind us in *The satanic verses* that the truest eye may now belong to the migrant's double vision; Toni Morrison's *Beloved* revives the past of slavery and its murderous rituals of possession and self-possession, in order to project a contemporary feminist fable of a woman's history and an emergent community of women.

What is striking about the 'new' internationalism is that the move from the specific to the general, from the material to the metaphoric, is not a smooth passage of transition and transcendence. The 'middle passage' of contemporary culture, as with slavery itself, is a process of displacement and disjunction that does not totalise experience. Increasingly, 'national' cultures are being produced from the perspective of disenfranchised minorities. The most significant effect of this process is not the proliferation of 'alternative histories of the excluded' producing, as some would have it, a pluralist anarchy. What my examples show is the changed basis for making international, postcolonial connections. The currency of critical comparativism, or aesthetic judgements, is no longer the sovereignty of the national culture conceived, as Benedict Anderson proposed, as an 'imagined community' rooted in a 'homogeneous empty time' of modernity and progress. The great connective narratives of capitalism and class drive the engines of social reproduction, but do not, in themselves, provide a foundational frame for those modes of cultural identification and political affect that form around issues of sexuality, race, feminism, the lifeworld of refugees or migrants, or the deathly social destiny of AIDS.

The testimony of my examples represents a revision in the concept of human community itself. What this geopolitical space may be, as a local and transnational reality, is being both interrogated and re-initiated. Feminism, in the 1990s, finds its solidarity not only in liberatory narratives of 'women's liberation' but in the painful ethical position of a slave woman, Morrison's Sethe in *Beloved*, who is pushed to infanticide; the body politic can no longer contemplate the nation's health as simply a civic virtue; it must rethink the question of rights for the entire national, and international, community from the AIDS perspective; the Western metropole must confront its postcolonial history, told by its influx of postwar migrants and refugees, as an indigenous or native narrative internal to its national identity; and the reason for this is made clear in the stammering, drunken words of Mr 'Whisky' Sisodia from *The satanic verses*: 'The trouble with the Engenglish is that their hiss hiss history happened overseas, so they dodo don't know what it means.' (Rushdie, 1988, p. 343)

Postcoloniality, for its part, is a salutary reminder of the persistent 'neo-colonial' relations within the 'new' world order and the multinational division of labour. Such a perspective enables the authentication of histories

26

of exploitation and the evolution of strategies of resistance. Beyond this, however, postcolonial critique bears witness to those countries and communities – in the North and the South, urban and rural – constituted 'otherwise than modernity'. Such cultures of a postcolonial contramodernity may be contingent to modernity, discontinuous or in contention with it, resistant to its oppressive, assimilatory technologies; but they also deploy the cultural hybridity of their borderline conditions to 'translate', and therefore reinscribe, the social imaginary of both metropolis and modernity. Listen to Guillermo Gomez-Pena:

hello America
this is the voice of *Gran Vato Charollero*
broadcasting from the hot deserts of Nogales, Arizona
zona de libre cogercio
2000 megaherz en todas direciones

you are celebrating Labor Day in Seattle
while the Klan demonstrates
against Mexicans in Georgia
ironia, 100% ironia
(Gomez-Pena, 1991)

Being in the 'beyond', then, is to inhabit an intervening space, as any dictionary will tell you. But to dwell 'in the beyond' is also, as I have shown, to be part of a revisionary time, a return to the present to redescribe our cultural contemporaneity; to reinscribe our human, historic commonality; to touch the future on its hither side. In that sense, then, the *intervening space* 'beyond', becomes *a space of intervention* in the here and now. To engage with such invention, and intervention, as Green and Gomez-Pena enact in their distinctive work, requires a sense of the new that resonates with the chicano aesthetic of *'rasquachismo'* as Tomas Ybarra-Frausto describes it: '...the utilization of available resources for syncretism, juxtaposition, and integration. *Rasquachismo* is a sensibility attuned to mixtures and confluence. (...) a delight in texture and sensuous surfaces (...) self-conscious manipulation of materials or iconography (...) the combination of found material and satiric wit (...) the manipulation of *rasquache* artifacts, codes and sensibilities from both sides of the border...' (Ybarra-Frausto, 1991, pp. 133-134)

The borderline work of art demands an encounter with 'newness' that is not part of the continuum of past and present; nor is it a 'newness' that can be contained in the mimesis of 'original and copy'. In both these cases, the image of the new is iconic rather than enunciatory; in both instances, cultural disjunction is represented as epistemological or mimetic distance. What is missing is the borderline sense of the new that is an insurgent act of cultural re-iteration. Such art does not merely recall the past as social cause or aesthetic precedent; it renews the past, refiguring it as a contingent 'in-between' space that innovates and interrupts the performance of the present. The 'past-present' is part of the necessity, not the nostalgia, of living.

Pepon Osorio's *objets trouvées* of the Nuyorican community – the statistics of infant mortality, or the silent (and silenced) spread of AIDS in the Hispanic community – are elaborated into baroque allegories of social alienation. But it is not the high drama of birth and death that captures Osorio's spectacular imagination. He is the great celebrant of the migrant act of survival, using his mixed-media works to make a hybrid cultural space that forms contingently, disjunctively, in the inscription of signs of cultural memory and sites of political agency. «La Cama» (The Bed) turns the highly decorated four-poster into the primal scene of lost-and-found childhood memories, the memorial to a dead nanny Juana, the *mise-en-scene* of the eroticism of the 'emigrant' everyday. Survival, for Osorio, is working in the interstices of a range of practices: the 'space' of installation, the spectacle of the social statistic, the transitive time of the body in performance.

For the 'newness' of the art of cultural translation is akin to that process of signification that Walter Benjamin describes as the 'foreignness of languages'. What Benjamin is referring to is the problem of representation 'native' to the production of the sign itself. Textual reference, the relation of the word to the concept, or the image to language, is an effect of the repetition and circulation of 'difference' (between signifier and signified, *énoncé* and *énonciation*, in the interstices of the discursive sign and its social symbol. Gary Hill's description of the signifying space of the electronic media, has a wider relevance to the figural construction of meaning itself: 'My work (...) has more to do with the relation of language and image. One tends to question the other. (...) It's not so much about duality, but about what happens in the middle. This is possible because of the electronic media. It really allows that reflexive space wherein both absence and presence take place.' (Hill, p. 39)

Through the notion of translation, 'foreignness' is embedded in the very syntax and temporality of cultural signification and communication. It is no longer adequate to think of cultural difference simply as an artistic or critical practice determined by external historical events such as migration or diaspora. Subaltern or minority cultures introduce this disjunctive notion of translational time into the very process by which artistic practices inscribe fundamental moments of social transformation deploying the dimensions of difference: inside/outside; past/present; difference/similitude; specificity/ generality. Social differences are not homogeneous under the sign of a 'reigning' category: race subsumed into class, gender into labour, sexuality into the ethics of the good life.

Such conditions of cultural displacement and political discrimination – where political victims become the best historical witnesses – are the grounds on which Frantz Fanon (1990), the Martinican psychoanalyst and participant in the Algerian revolution, locates an agency of empowerment: 'As soon as I desire I am asking to be considered. I am not merely here-and-now, sealed into thingness. I am for somewhere else and for something else. I demand that notice be taken of my negating activity insofar as I pursue something other than life; in so far as I do battle for the creation of a human world – that is a world of reciprocal recognitions. (p. 218) (...) I should constantly remind myself that the real leap consists in introducing invention into existence. In the world in which I travel, I am endlessly creating myself. (p. 229) (...) And it is by going beyond the historical, instrumental hypothesis that I will initiate my cycle of freedom.' (p. 231)

Once more, the desire for recognition, 'for somewhere else, for something else' that takes the experience of history *beyond* the instrumental hypothesis. Once again, the space of intervention emerging in the cultural interstices that introduce creative invention into existence. And one last time, a return to the performance of identity as iteration, the re-creation of the self in the world of travel, the re-settlement of the borderline community of migration. Fanon recognises the crucial importance, for subordinated peoples, of asserting their indigenous cultural traditions and retrieving their repressed histories. But he is far too aware of the dangers of the fixity and fetishism of identities within the calcification of colonial cultures to recommend that 'roots' be struck in the celebratory romance of the past or by homogenising the history of the present. The negating activity is, indeed, the intervention of the 'beyond' that establishes a boundary, a bridge, where 'presencing' begins.

To be recognised for my negating activity is to be valued for my power to 'make' a difference rather than to reflect it; it is to be accepted for my contradictory, contentious collaboration, rather than my collusive, predictable presence. I want to be recognised for the force with which I can explore the limits of my identities, the ends of my institutions. I want to be valued for the amnesia of my history, the contingency of my cultures, the silence of my languages, the boundaries of my body, the miasma of my memories – and in that reach beyond, I want to touch your histories and silences, configure our cultural confusions, meld memories of what remains untranslatable but no less telling.

Once, as a boy in Bombay, no more than ten or twelve, I opened a museum catalogue and discovered a late Giacometti. The attenuated figure, stilled in the petrified forest of his body, the straitened flesh turned inwards: who was this man? And suddenly the museum opened onto a thousand village squares and city centres, in every part of India, where the main street or the arterial road leads to a familiar, diminutive piece of statuary. A meagre man, naked to the bone, legs like hollowed bamboos, buttocks like empty dugs, the icon of Independent India: Mahatma Gandhi.

From that moment on, for me, the Father of the Nation lived in the shadow of Giacometti's «Walking Man 1» (1960). And when I read of the Mahatma's defiant march to the seashore at Dandi, to draw a handful of free salt from the water and thus oppose the British Government's iniquitous salt tax, I saw the other figure marching too: the walking man, stooped, deliberate, but carrying himself and his mission with a certain lightness of being.

In that walk, that hither and thither, that turns salt into the symbol of freedom, or bronze into a human image, I felt the need to translate, to create something else, somewhere between art and history; and with it the desire to go *beyond*...

30

2 Nomads in a transformed Europe: Figurations for an alternative consciousness *

Rosi Braidotti

'Chi è ciascuno di noi, se non una combinatoria d'esperienze, d'informa-zioni, di letture, d'immaginazioni? Ogni vita è un'enciclopedia, una biblioteca, un inventario d'oggetti, un campionario di stili, dove tutto puo essere continuamente immescolato e rioridnato in tutti i modi possibili' Italo Calvino, *Lezioni americane*. (1988, p. 120)

The polyglot is a linguistic nomad. The polyglot is a specialist of the treacherous nature of language, of any language. Words have a way of not standing still, of following their own ways. They come and go, pursuing pre-set semantic trials, leaving behind acoustic, graphic or unconscious traces. In *Alice in Wonderland*, Humpty Dumpty sagaciously reminds us that all that counts in defining the meaning of words is who is the boss. This remark always struck me as peculiary apt for a person like me, who is constantly in-between different languages.

I was born in Italy, more specifically on that stretch of North-Eastern land that the Venetians colonised way back in the thirteenth and fourteenth centuries. Venice was created under the sign of nomadism, when the local people took to the water, in a flight from Attila the Hun and his mighty warriors. It was to provide a steady flow of globetrotters, not the least known of whom, Marco Polo, still shines on as one of the world's greatest decoders of foreign signs.

I was subsequently raised in Australia's polycultural metropoles, just before the trend of 'multiculturalism' became fashionable. Contact with Aboriginal culture was nonexistent, but their absence rang to my ears as a

* Sections of this article were previously published under the title: 'United States of Europe or United Colours of Benetton?' *Differences* 2, no 3.

constant, unspoken sign of inner turmoil within the Australian psyche and way of life. It made me feel very uncomfortable.

I wrote my first substantial academic piece, my doctoral dissertation, in French at the Sorbonne, in a post-1968 climate where the philosophy classes, especially Gilles Deleuze's, attracted more foreigners – British, Iranians, Cambodians, Algerians, Australians, Cameroonians, etc. – than local students. I subsequently moved in and out of the Italian, French and English language – in its British, Australian, American and other variations – not in straight lines, but rather by an infinitely shifting scale of degrees of hybridisation. Even when I decided to settle for the English language as the main vehicle of expression, it only resulted in a web of hyphenated English dialects: 'Italo-Australian', 'Franglais', New Yorkese, Parisian patois, 'Dutch-lish' and many others. With the move to the Netherlands in 1988, this shifting land-scape settled into a life-style based on the permanence of temporary arrangements and the comfort of contingent foundations.

Over the years, I have developed a relationship of great fascination towards mono-lingual people: those who were born into the symbolic system in the one language that was to remain theirs for the rest of their life. Come to think of it, I do not know many people like that, but I do believe they exist, at least, I can easily imagine them. Sometimes, as I walk down the street, I believe I can actually see some of them: people comfortably established in the illusion of familiarity which their 'mother tongue' gives them. Had they read Lacan, they would know that there is no such a thing as a mother tongue, that all tongues carry the name of the father and are stamped by its register. Psychoanalysis also teaches us the irreparable loss of a sense of steady origin, which accompanies the acquisition of language, of any language. Had they heard Homi Bhabha or George Steiner, they would know that the state of translation is the common condition of all thinking beings. But most people do not think this way.

All around us, in this culture of end of millennium, the belief in the importance, the God-given seriousness and foundational value of mother tongues is ever so strong. In this new Europe that witnesses all of its old problems, in a wave of return of the repressed that is disconcerting to say the least, in this ethnocentric fortress, the concept of the mother tongue is stronger than ever. It feeds into the renewed and exacerbated sense of nationalism, regionalism, localism, which marks this particular moment of our history.

The polyglot surveys this situation with the greatest critical distance; a person who is in-transit between the languages, neither here nor there, knows better than to believe in steady identities and mother tongues. Tell me, is it because of their mother tongues that women in Bosnia Herzegovina and Croatia are being systematically raped and held in procreative concentration camps? Is cohercive motherhood by gang-rape the price to pay for speaking the 'wrong' mother tongue? Is not every appeal to the 'right' mother tongue the matrix of terror, of fascism, of despair? And tell me again, is it because the polyglot practices a sort of gentle promiscuity with different linguistic bedrocks, that s/he has long since relinquished any notion of linguistic or ethnic purity?

There are no mother tongues, just linguistic sites one takes her/his starting point from. The polyglot has no vernacular, but many lines of transit, of transgression; some common habits are lost on her/him, for instance, to be able to recall in what language s/he chants nursery rhymes, in what language s/he dreams, loves or fantasises. The complex muscular and mental apparati that join forces in the production of language combine in the polyglot to produce strange sounds, phonetic connections, vocal combinations and rhythmical junctions. A sort of polymorphous perversity accompanies a polyglot's capacity to slip in-between the languages, stealing acoustic traces here, dipthong-sounds there, in a constant and child-like game of persiflage. The best gift to give anyone, but especially a polyglot, is a new word, a word s/he does not know yet.

The polyglot knows that the word is the symbolic glue that links us together in a tenuous and yet workable web of mediated misunderstandings, which we call civilisation. The polyglot knows that language is not only and not even the instrument of communication, but a site of symbolic exchange. Since Freud and Nietzsche, the Western world should know that meaning does not coincide with consciousness, that there is a non-conscious foundation to most of our actions: *cogito ergo sum* is the madness of the West, its downfall, its folly. No one is master in their house: *desidero ergo sum* is a more accurate depiction of the process of making meaning.

In other words, a fundamental imbalance exists between the libidinal or affective grounds and the symbolic forms available to express them. *'C'est du même endroit, que l'on sait et l'on ignore'* – it is from the same location that you can both see and fail to see. All knowledge is situated, that is to say partial; we are all stuttering for words, even when we speak 'fluently'.

Quoting Spinoza and Nietzsche, the philosopher Gilles Deleuze (1974) banks on the affective substratum as a force capable of freeing us from hegemonic habits of thinking. Affectivity in this scheme is prediscursive: desire is not only unconscious but it remains nonthought at the very heart of our thought, because it is that which sustains the very activity of thinking. Our desires are that which evades us, in the very act of propelling us forth, leaving as the only indicator of *who* we are, the traces of *where* we have already been, that is to say, of what we have already ceased to be. What matters therefore is how to resist the recoding of the subject in/as yet another sovereign, self-representational language. Nomadism is neither a rhetorical gesture nor a mere figure of speech, but a political and epistemological necessity for critical cultural action at the end of this century.

The polyglot knows intimately what Saussure teaches explicitly: that the connection between linguistic signs is arbitrary. The arbitrariness of language, experienced over several languages, is enough to drive one to relativist despair. Thus, the polyglot becomes the prototype of the post-psychoanalytic speaking subject: struck by the maddening, fulminating insight about the arbitrariness of linguistic meanings, and yet resisting the free fall into cynicism. To be able to see this, and still not jump to the conclusion that any-thing goes, that arbitrary does not equate with absurd and polyvalence does not mean anarchy. That the interchangeability of signs is not a medieval death dance, but a pattern of orchestrated repetitions. That one must respect the complexity, not drown in it. The polyglot is an ethical entity, confronting complexity and yet avoiding relativism.

The polyglot practices an aesthetics based on compassion for the incon-gruities, the repetitions, the arbitrariness of the languages s/he deals with. Writing is, for the polyglot, a process of undoing the illusory stability of fixed identities, bursting open the bubble of ontological security that comes from familiarity with one linguistic site. The polyglot exposes this false security as the site of the incest fantasy: s/he is Christa Wolf's Cassandra: 'So far, every-thing that has befallen me has struck an answering chord. This is the secret that encircles me and holds me together: there is something of everyone in me, so I have belonged completely to no one, and I have even understood their hatred of me.' (Wolf, 1984) Writing in this mode is about disengaging the sedentary nature of words, destabilising common-sensical meanings, deconstructing established forms of consciousness.

In this respect, writers can be polyglots within the same language; you can speak English and write many different Englishes. What else did the great modernists like Virginia Woolf, Gertrude Stein or my least favourite: James

Joyce do, but invent a new English dialect? What else are Alice Walker and Toni Morrison doing but redesigning the boundaries of the citadel that was English? Becoming a polyglot in your own mother tongue: that is writing. Nomadism: vertiginous progression towards deconstructing the self; molecularisation of the self.

The polyglot writer despises the huge traffic jams of meanings waiting at the city gates for admission into the realm of sense: the pollution of established meanings. Nomadic writing longs, instead, for the areas of silence, in-between the official cacophonies: this is the voice of radical non-belonging, of outsidedness. The rest is silence.

Writing is not only a process of constant translation, but also of successive adaptations to different cultural realities. This is a difficult task that translates into the need to take your bearings, to contextualise your utterances, to draw maps, in a mobile manner. As an intellectual style, nomadism consists not so much in being homeless, as in being capable of recreating your home everywhere or anywhere. The nomad carries her/his essential belongings with her/him wherever s/he goes and can recreate a home base anywhere.

I think that many of the things I write are cartographies, that is to say a sort of intellectual landscape gardening that gives me a horizon, a frame of reference within which I can set up my own theoretical tent. The nomad and the cartographer proceed hand in hand, because they share a situational need, except that the nomad knows how to read invisible maps, or maps written in the wind, on the stones, in the flora. The globetrotting writer Bruce Chatwin, in *The Songlines* (1988) shows admirably the extent to which the nomad's identity, in Gypsies, Australian Aborigines and other tribes, consists in memorising oral poetry, which is an elaborate and accurate description of the territories that need to be crossed in the nomad's never-ending journey. A totemic geography marks this sort of identity. The desert is a gigantic map of signs, for those who know how to read them, for those who can sing their way through the wilderness.

Italo Calvino, the Italian writer who spent most of his life in Paris, in *Le città invisibili* (1972) has the hero Marco Polo displaying the nomadic skill of memorising imperceptible maps. Marco Polo reads the chessboard on which he is playing with the Kublai Khan. From a small scratch in the wooden board, he is capable of reconstructing its genealogy, tracing the sort of the trees it was made from, their origin and structure, down to the kind of craftsmanship that was used to make it. The map is invisible or rather it is available only to those who have been trained to read invisible ink signs.

Luce Irigaray, a Belgian-born philosopher who lives in France as an immigrant within the same language and is most followed and understood in Italy (where the Communist Party appointed her as advisor), carefully notes in her latest books the place and the date where she wrote each article. I appreciate the cartographic precision and see it as a sort of situated ethics. Were I to do the same, I would have to note down places like: Jyvaskula in central Finland, Melbourne in south-western Australia, Verona in northern Italy, Utrecht in central Netherlands and so on. This mode of writing also involves conversations and exchanges with other transmobile entities, foreigners without whom the intellectual life in the many metropoles of the world would come to an end: Americans in Paris; Dutch and Australian everywhere; African-Americans, Italo-Americans and other hyphenated subjects: Jewish Americans and Jewish Parisians, postcolonial British and Israelis.

Without such geographical dislocations, I could not write at all and what I write is *not* travel literature. But I do have special affection for the places of transit that go with travelling: stations and airport lounges, trams, shuttle buses and check-in areas. In-between zones where all ties are suspended and time stretched to a sort of continuous present. Oases of non-belonging, spaces of detachment. No-(wo)man's lands.

Maybe this is why these open, public spaces of transition are privileged sites of creation for contemporary artists.[*] At the «Decade Show», which was held at the New Museum of Contemporary Art in New York in 1990, the artist Martha Rozler exhibited an installation piece called «In the place of the public» (1983-1990), which consisted of large photographs of places of passage, especially airport lounges and luggage carrousels, accompanied by extensive comments inspired by the Marxist philosopher Henri Lefebvre. In Rozler's vision, public spaces are sites that mark rites of passage, subjected to culture-specific imperatives such as schedules; rhythms of production; allowed or forbidden directions; loading and unloading; areas of transition and spaces of transactions. Space is an abstraction ruled by the logic of the market economy and, as such, it is 'permeated with social relations'. The great merit of Rozler's art is to have captured both aspects of these areas of transit: their instrumental value as well as their peculiar anonymity. Airport lounges are places where one passes 'without registering passage', as such they are a

[*]   I am grateful to Juul Hymans, of Radio Mundo, for helping me to formulate this insight.

microcosmos of contemporary society which, as Frederic Jameson suggests, may well be 'post-industrial, but it nevertheless displays a more pure, that is to say a more ruthless form of capitalism than ever before'.

Installations in public spaces, in areas of passing through, are also central to the work of other important contemporary women artists. For instance, Barbara Krueger's large billboards are strategically set up in huge intersections at the centre of the metropoles of the Western world. They announce 'We don't need another hero' and 'Surveillance is their busywork' with breathtaking force. In these days of postindustrial decay of the urban space, artists like Krueger manage to return to the artwork both the monumental value that used to be its prerogative in the past, while also preserving its politically committed nature. Krueger's punchy messages are invigorating also for their powerfully feminist touch.

Similarly, Jenny Holzer's electronic panels flash right across the advertisement-infested skyline of our cities and relay very politicised and consciousness-raising messages: 'Money creates taste', 'Property created crime', 'Torture is barbaric', etc. etc. Holzer also uses the airport spaces, especially the information panels of luggage carrousels, to transmit her staggering messages, such as: 'Lack of charisma can be fatal', and ironical ones, such as: 'If you had behaved nicely, the communists wouldn't exist' or: 'What country should you adopt if you hate poor people?'

Rozler, Krueger and Holzer are perfect examples of postmodern, insightful and non-nostalgic appropriations of public spaces for creative and political purposes. In their hands, areas of transit and passage become contemporary equivalents of the desert, not only because of the enormous, alienating solitude that characterises them, but also because they are heavily marked by signs and boards indicating a multitude of possible directions, to which the artist adds her own unexpected and disruptive one.

The urban space is thus one huge map that requires special skills of decoding and interpreting; in the hands of these artists the city also becomes text, signifying artifact. The public spaces as sites of creativity therefore highlight a paradox: they are both loaded with signification and profoundly anonymous; they are spaces of detached transition, but also venues of inspiration, of visionary insight, of great release of creativity. Brian Eno's musical experiment with «Music for airports» makes the same point very strongly: it is a creative appropriation of the dead heart of the slightly hallucinating zones that are the places of transit.

I remember, however, landing at Paris international airport and seeing all of this in-between area occupied by immigrants from various parts of the former French empire: they had arrived, but were not allowed entry, so they camped in these luxurious transit zones, waiting. The dead, panoptical heart of the new EC will scrutinize them and not allow them in easily: it is crowded at the margins and non-belonging can be hell.

At times and in spite of all reasonable evidence to the contrary, a sort of euphoric rhetoric accompanies the push for a new European spirit: '...the winds of freedom are blowing again, after the end of the cold war, and the continent of Europe stands up again, united at last, ready to face the challenges of its American and Japanese competitors...' One does not even have to read between the lines to detect, in this kind of rhetoric, the influence of economic interests and the vicious cercle of the market economy. In this respect, the colossal success – at least here in Europe – of Benetton's advertising campaign seems to sum up the semiotic code of the European unification project: all united in our respective differences, provided that our currency is the same, our living standards comparable, and our designer-clothes, of course, made (in off-shore production) in Italy (with capital held transcontinentally). (Spivak, 1987) One need not be cynical about the new European community. Nevertheless, some questions do spring to mind, and the nomadic intellectual may wish to inject a dose of healthy suspicion into the rhetoric of the united-Europe project.

What can one, in fact, plead in favour of European consciousness? Christa Wolf: 'The fact that it was Europeans who, by subjugating and exploiting other people and continents, learned – or confirmed – that consciousness of mastery and race which determined the direction of technological development (including weapon technology), as well as the structures of the economy and of nations? The fact that we ourselves brought into the world the forces which threaten us?' (Wolf, 1984)

The polyglot nomadic intellectual in Europe, today, must provide food for thought about the exclusionary, ethnocentric usage that is currently being made of the notion of a common European community. As far back as 1938 Virginia Woolf was raising the issue: 'As a woman I have no country, as a woman I want no country, as a woman my country is the whole world.' The identification of female identity with a sort of planetary exile has since become a *topos* of feminist studies, with writers like the Algerian-born, Jewish Parisian Hélène Cixous (1975) and the Belgian-French Luce Irigaray (1977) stressing this point.

38

I see a danger, however, in this metaphor of exile: being 'a citizen of the world' may seem attractive at first, but it can also be an evasive tactic. As if all women had in common a sense of their home-lessness, country-lessness, of *not* having a common anchoring point. How satisfactory is this both as a diagnosis of the status of women in 1993 and as a vision of the role of women? As Alice Walker (1984) pointed out in her response to Virginia Woolf: is this nonchalant detachment not the privilege of caste and Whiteness? What could it mean to people who have never had a home, or a remembered home country, like the slave girl in the USA? Is the lofty metaphor of planetary exile not very ethnocentric? In this end of century, when Europe and other parts of the world are confronted by the problem of refugees from the East and the South and movements of populations away from war-torn homelands into exile and when the right to belong, the right to enter, the right to asylum, are too serious an issue to be merely metaphorised.

As a matter of fact, I think that part of the problem lies in the habit that consists in metaphorising certain conditions, such as the exile, the migrant, the homeless and others. The process of metaphorisation implies an instrumental use of the people or experiences involved, that I find particularly offensive. This is why, in my work, I prefer to work with the notion of figuration. This also implies that, in my estimate, at this particular point in time, the creative minds, especially the artists, are in a stronger position than the theorists to find alternative forms of representation for changing realities.

A figuration is no metaphor, but rather a figural (as opposed to 'figurative') mode of expressing differences. A figuration works by expression, not by displacement or appropriation, which is typical of the metaphorical mode. A figuration works by evoking mental associations, by arousing memories and traces. In some cases, the figural mode functions according to what I have called 'the philosophy of as if'. It is *as if* some experiences were reminiscent or evocative of others. This ability to flow from one set of experiences to another is a quality of interconnectedness that I praise highly.

Drawing a flow of connections need not be an appropriative, rapacious way to proceed, quite on the contrary: Deleuze practices it as an 'intensive' theoretical mode. Laurie Anderson's performance-art is a great example of nomadic style, in the 'as-if' mode (Howell, 1992, p. 17): situations and people are always reversable in Anderson's conceptual universe. This constant flow of experience allows Laurie Anderson to depict a high-tech kind of continuum between different levels of experience, which in turn makes for her extraordinary capacity to evoke the paradox of a complexity that rests on a minimalist approach.

Next to this, another figuration I want to emphasise is that of the migrant. The migrant is no exile: s/he has a clear destination: s/he goes from one point in space to another for a very clear purpose. Europe today is not a lily-white culture: the phenomenon of economic migration, especially from the Near East and the Mediterranean area, and the postcolonial parts of the globe, has created in every European city a set of foreign 'subcultures'. In these, women usually play the role of the loyal keepers of the original home culture: they constitute the bulk of the 'domestic foreigners'. How close are the 'White' intellectual women to the migrant women who have even fewer citizen rights than we have? How sensitive are we to the intellectual potential of the foreigners that we have right here, in our own back yard? This problem is all the more urgent at a time of increasing racism and xenophobia and revival of nationalistic ideologies.

The image of female migrancy can be complemented by that of the nomad: I shall take the nomad as the prototype of the 'man or woman of ideas' (Spender, 1982). As Deleuze emphasises, the point of being an intellectual nomad is about crossing boundaries, about the act of going, regardless of the destination. 'The life of the nomad is the intermezzo (...) He is a vector of deterritorialization' (Deleuze and Guattari, 1986). The nomad enacts transitions without a teleological purpose.

The history of ideas is always a nomadic story: the physical displacement is just a way of preserving in time certain ideas, so that they do not get lost. Ideas are as mortal as human beings and as subjected as we are to the crazy twists and turns of history. Without international escape routes, for instance, neither psychoanalysis nor Marxism would have survived the lethal impact and the horrors of European fascism and Nazism. In a feminist perspective the figure of the nomad, as opposed to the exile, allows us to think of international dispersion and dissemination of ideas as forms of resistance, as ways of preserving ideas which may otherwise have been condemned to wilful obliteration or to collectively produced amnesia.

Faced with these issues, I suggest that feminists and other critical intellectuals today cultivate a nomadic consciousness. Their challenge is how to conjugate the positive aspects of the multilayered international or multicultural perspective, with responsibility for and accountability to their gender.

40

Important to this is a confrontation of the many differences that separate and distinguish women among themselves. No planetary exiles, feminists today should be locally situated political subjects. The emphasis thus placed on situated perspectives, which I borrow from Donna Haraway (1990), allows us to respect cultural diversity without falling into cheap relativism. It allows feminists to think of the differences among women, without losing sight of the commonalities of their gender. The crucial question here is: how is this awareness of differences likely to affect the often fragile alliance of women of different classes, races, ages and sexual preferences?

Following Haraway, I think that one of the ways in which we could visualise a multidifferentiated and multisituated feminist perspective is through the image of multiple literacies, i.e.: a collective nascent polyglot. That is to say, we need to become fluent in a variety of styles, disciplinary angles in many different languages. Relinquishing the dream of sisterhood in favour of the recognition of the complexity of the semiotic and material conditions in which we operate. In this approach, cultural differences become the basis for communication and not the stuff that divides us.

I believe that this redefinition of the subject[*] starts with the revaluation of the bodily roots of subjectivity, rejecting the traditional vision of the knowing subject as universal, neutral, and consequently gender-free. This 'positional' or situated way of seeing the subject states that the most important location or situation is the rooting of the subject into the spatial frame of the body. The first and foremost of locations in reality is one's own embodiment. Rethinking the body as our primary situation is the starting point for the epistemological side of the nomadic consciousness.

The body, or the embodiment of the subject, is a key term, which need not be understood as either a biological or a sociological category, but rather as a point of overlapping between the physical, the symbolic, and the sociological. In other words, the starting point for creative redefinitions of subjectivity is paradoxical: it is a new form of materialism that develops the notion of corporeal materiality of the poststructuralists, by emphasising the embodied and therefore sexually differentiated structure of the speaking subject. The subject thus defined is not a monolithic essence defined once and for all, but rather the site of multiple, complex, and potentially contradictory sets of experience, defined by overlapping variables, such as class, race, age,

---

[*]   I borrow this expression from Teresa de Lauretis, *Alice doesn't*. Bloomington, Indiana University Press, 1984.

41

life style, sexual preference, and others.

Laurie Anderson's strange angels of history – stolen from Walter Benjamin – are for me a perfect figuration of the kind of consciousness I am trying to theorise and defend. Laurie Anderson's performance art is a way of displacing her physical factuality. Anderson's presence is technologically mediated to such an extent that, the closer we get to her, like being able to hear the sound of her heartbeat, the more she recedes into the distance. Anderson's body is not one, but a shifting horizon of technologically mediated transitions. This picture reflects for me the poststructuralist analysis of the simultaneous overexposure and disappearance of the body in contemporary culture. On top of this, Anderson's mediated selves are also a strategy aiming at displacing our expectations about the female body as object of display or spectacle: in this respect she blurs masterfully gender boundaries.

On the artistic level, the distinction I am defending between the migrant, the exile and the nomad, corresponds to different genres and to different relationships to time.

The mode and tense of exile style are based on an acute sense of foreignness, coupled with the often hostile perception of the host country. Exile literature is marked by a sense of loss or separation from the home country, which, often for political reasons, is a lost horizon. Memory, recollection, and the rumination of acoustic traces of the mother tongue is central to this literary genre, as in Nathalie Sarraute's *Enfance*, for instance. Translated into time, this genre favours a sort of flow of reminiscence, which I would translate into a sort of future perfect: 'it will have been like this...'.

The migrant, on the other hand, is caught in an in-between state whereby the narrative of the origin has the effect of destabilising the present. Migrant literature is about a suspended, often impossible present; it is about missing, nostalgia, and blocked horizons. The past acts as a burden in migrant literature: it is a fossilised definition of language, which marks the lingering of the past into the present. The Italo-Australian writer Rosa Capiello offers a great example of this in her devastating response to an all-time Australian classical text, which she calls: *Oh, Lucky Country!* Postcolonial literature is not a migrant genre. In her analysis of Salman Rushdie's *The satanic verses*, Gayatri Spivak further distinguishes between the migrant and the postcolonial immigrant, and warns us against privileging the metropolitan migrancy over the postcolonial condition. (1990, pp. 41-60)

42

The nomadic consciousness, on the other hand, is akin to what Foucault called countermemory, it is a form of resisting assimilation or homologation into dominant ways of representing the self. The feminist or critical intellectual as nomad is someone who forgot to forget injustice and symbolic poverty: her memory is activated against the stream; she enacts a rebellion of subjugated knowledges. The nomadic tense is the imperfect: it is active, continuous; the nomadic trajectory is controlled speed: Isabelle Eberhardt's cross-dressing herself into freedom of movement. The nomadic style is about transitions and passages without predetermined destinations or lost homelands.

Last, but not least, there is a privileged link between the nomad and violence. From the dawn of time, nomadic tribes have been what Deleuze calls 'war machines', that is to say perfectly trained armed bands. The raids, the sacking of the cities, the looting, the killing of the sedentary population are the nomad's answer to agriculture.

The central figuration here is the opposition of the city to the space of the desert; Bruce Chatwin describes the city as a garden superimposed on a sheepfold: a space of agriculture and sheep farming. (1988) As such, it is diametrically opposed to the open space: the *noumos*, or plot of land, which is the etymological root of 'nomad', which means the chief of clan elder who supervises the allocation of pastures to the tribe. By extension, *nomos* came to mean the law; thus, we get terms like *nemesis*, which means appropriate or divine justice. Almost all monetary expressions also come from this pastoral origin: *nomisma* means current coins, from which we get numismatics. The words meaning money – like pecuniary – have the root in the word for sheep: *pecu/pecus*.

Deleuze confirms: *noumos* is a principle of distribution of the land, as such it came to represent the opposition of the power of the *polis*, because it was a space without enclosures or borders. It was the pastoral open nomadic space in opposition to which the sedentary powers of the city was erected. Metropolitan space versus nomadic trajectories.

Nomadic violence is consequently opposed to state apparatus violence: the tribe is the counterarmy, it is the terrorist unit. Is this why nomads have always been persecuted by the state, as dangerous criminals? Is this why so many Romany people were killed in concentration camps? Was it fear of their mobility that stiffened the murderous hand around their neck? I remember my grandfather – a respected leader of the antifascist resistance – warning me that 'Gypsies steal children'. I remember looking at the first Romany people who came through my town – which is barely 100 kilometres from the Yugoslavian border – with fascination and fear: did they really steal children? Would they steal me? Where would I end up, if they stole me? All of a sudden, that fear taught me that the road, the old familiar road that opened in front of my family home, was an irresistible path which could lead as far as Melbourne, Paris, or Utrecht. That stepping on it could be fatal, as it turned out to be.

From Kleist's depiction of Panthesilea, in the homonymous play, to the legend of Medea, other forms of violence also come into focus in female nomads: a sort of rough encounter with hostile environmental forces; the emphasis on physical resistance and stamina; the reliance on rituals and dramas, in the absence of the temple of established religion. There is a rigorous, relentless sort of toughness in the nomad: they are not *only* nice.

This redefinition of the creative subject as a multiple, complex process is also an attempt to avoid relativism and to rethink the unity of the subject, without reference to humanistic beliefs, without dualistic oppositions, linking instead body and mind in a new flux of self.

In other words, in my view, there cannot be lasting social change or meaningful contemporary creativity without the construction of new kinds of desiring subjects as molecular, nomadic, and multiple. I take it as the task of the artists, as well as of other critical intellectuals, to have the courage to face complexity, differences, and the absolute loss of monolithic schemes of thought. For as the American artist Martha Rozler put it: 'There cannot be fragments where there is no whole.'

3   Towards 2000:

Diversity, identity and the arts

Lola Young

What do popular images tell us about the concept of cultural diversity in the late twentieth century? Popular culture – music, television, magazines, advertisements – indicates, on the one hand, the visibility of Black[*] people in Western European culture at the same time as representing Blackness as exotic, 'other', endowed with natural rhythm, sporting ability and so on, and masking the way in which we are consistently marginalised and invisibilised where it really matters: in those labyrinthine corridors of power. With the celebrations in recognition of the birth of the New Europe, ethnicity, 'race' and national consciousness are issues that are in need of urgent attention. In the space available to me, I want to raise some questions and problematics in relation to the politics of 'race', cultural theory and the arts.

The attempt to represent nations as consisting of culturally homogeneous communities in which a sense of patriotic belonging exists is a pervasive and crucial source of moral and political ideas. The idea that a homogeneous national identity has ever existed anywhere, is, of course, highly questionable, since there have always been schisms along class, regional, and gender lines. Also the part that mass migration – both in the past and currently – has played in the formation of national cultures and identities has been consistently denied. However, the notion of national identity may be invoked to mobilise support for neo-imperialist military activities or in order to divert attention away from the inadequate policies of governments which are unable to deal with the effects of the economic system they support – the effects of recession, unemployment, homelessness, crime and disaffection. The rallying call is for those who can lay claim to a common national heritage to pull

---

[*]   There is a difficulty regarding terminology here: rather than list those whom I am
including in the term 'Black', I will just say that, in this context, it is similar to the
American phrase 'people of colour' and is not confined to those of Black African or Asian
descent.

together and defeat any enemies within.

In the late sixties, through the evocation of England as a New Jerusalem whose 'green and pleasant lands' were being threatened with hordes of savage immigrants, Enoch Powell, a Conservative Member of Parliament at the time, was able to tap into the vast resources of White racism in Britain. His pronouncements have to be considered in the context of the demise of the British Empire and the establishment of relatively autonomous former colonies. The presence of Black people in Britain has served to problematise the notion of national identity, Englishness or Britishness, and the relationship of those terms to Black people. Similarly, the expanded Europe with its presumption of Whiteness is disrupted by the presence of people of colour.

The notion that Europe is a continent without frontiers rings hollow to many: the boundaries are those of nation, of skin colour or 'race', of ethnicity, of gender, of culture. It is significant that this united, frontierless community of Europe cannot bring itself to declare, explicitly, that racism is illegal. Community nationals and their families are protected from discriminatory practices but those who fall outside of this imagined community are not. I am not suggesting that legislation in itself prevents racism but it forces a space whereby the issue has to be discussed. It is hard to be antiracist when racism as such is not acknowledged.

Racism itself, in Europe, is not a homogeneous but a fractured field of activities, behaviours, attitudes, and practices that is comprised of anti-Jewish, anti-Turk, anti-Asian, anti-Muslim, anti-African (further subdivided into North African and sub-Saharan), anti-Romany, and anti-other positions. I am not going to attempt to define racism, instead, I am being inclusive rather than exclusive when I use the term and will not differentiate between its various forms. I would also like to point out that racism is gendered in terms of the way that it constructs the notions of femininity and masculinity in different manners: culture is gendered and the way in which racism operates may be experienced differently by women and men. We are brought up in a cultural, social, and political context in which masculine behaviours are defined as being distinct from feminine, and attributes of Blackness are distinguished from Whiteness. Racism needs to be reinserted into theoretical discussions because, I feel, the process of identifying and deconstructing essentialism and ethnic absolutism has assisted in the effacement of the lived experience of racism from sustained examination in cultural theory and analysis.

We are facing a complex historical conjuncture in which issues of identity are in a continual state of flux. The question of whether current theoretical frameworks are adequate to the task of analysing the particular historical moment which we are experiencing needs to be addressed. Debates within the academy or in the relatively rarefied atmosphere of conferences about postmodernism, poststructuralism and postcolonialism, are often seen as having nothing to do with, or to contribute to, the understanding of the crises which Black people face. However, whilst there are profound difficulties with thinking about current cultural theory as a way into a radical politics of transformation, the notion that ideas which critically engage with culture and aesthetics are not relevant to Black people needs intense probing.

The field of critical cultural theory and discourse is dominated by White males who still seem to be unaware that people of colour – particularly Black women – exist in the field of cultural production and criticism. Where White feminists have made interventions, they too have constructed a space which is largely exclusive of Black women. However, it should be acknowledged that there has been some fruitful exchanging of words between theory and practice and certainly Black, feminist, lesbian, and gay image-makers have drawn on theoretical insights as diverse as semiotics, psychoanalysis, and post-modernism and used these strategies to consciously inform their work. What is significant about postmodernist theoretical positions, in particular, is the claim to have widened the critical and theoretical terrain to include and legitimate discussions of Otherness and difference. However, in Britain and North America at least, postmodernism rarely engages with slavery, colonial-ism, and imperialism, the racial politics of which are a fundamental part of Western European history, although this is not often acknowledged to be so.

The roots of postmodernity lie in the Age of Reason and it is important to critically examine the terms of that legacy. The Age of Reason – otherwise known as the Age of Scientific Racism or the Age of Genocide – and its bequest implicates every country in Europe in epistemological, psychological, and physical violence. The heritage of the Age of Europe is highly ambiguous. It was a political project which expanded the boundaries of knowledge and thought in technology, science and philosophy – contributing so much to the development of the world at the same time as leaving a trail of destruction through so many of its peoples.

A radical approach to postmodernism would entail practitioners and critics working together to disrupt institutionalised discrimination in the academy, in establishment art galleries and museums, and in media

47

institutions, through identification with those who are subjected to, and oppressed by, discriminatory processes and practices due to 'race', gender, physical disabilities, sexuality, age, and so on. There is still potential for alliances to be made in the shared sense of alienation and fragmentation which characterises what has come to be known as the postmodern existence for many people.

This clearly presents a challenge to us all, not least because frequently, in order to be in a position to mount such a challenge to established discursive practices, those who engage with cultural and racial politics and identity find themselves in a position whereby they are financially dependent on those whose power and authority they seek to overturn, whose mechanisms for sustaining power they struggle to undermine. Cultural workers need to articulate specific objectives and targets and to establish supportive networks so that the potential empowerment through sharing sensibilities which interconnect class, gender and race oppression may be realised. Commitment and solidarity around a clearly articulated programme for change are the fundamental issues.

Let us examine the issue of cultural identity through an interrogation of the relationship between Black people and history, and think about the place of history in our struggles. Contemporary critical discourses suggest that the moment of static individual identities is over – if indeed it ever existed – and thus, the basis for forming groupings on notions of fixed identities cannot be sustained. Yet the term 'Black' still has considerable political currency. In addition, diaspora is frequently invoked by Black people of African descent – and increasingly by those of Asian descent – involved in creating various cultural forms, practices and theoretical work. There is a desire to semantically bind African-Caribbeans, African-Americans, and Black cultural activists in Britain, to a symbolic conceptualisation of Africa and diaspora. Crucial to making cultural connections is the sense of a shared past. Continuity and knowledge of traditions was of course distorted and disrupted by slavery, colonialism and imperialism, and history – defined in a particular way – has effectively become the prerogative of European societies: a marker of alleged cultural, intellectual, and moral superiority. It is important, therefore, not to abandon the past: we still have to struggle for those silenced in history to be heard. That is not the same as fetishising the past; it is politicising and expanding the notion of history.

48

Access to history has been denied to us but not without resistance and contestation. Recent debates about Black people and history have centred around absences and invisibility, and cultural activists have sought to redress the imbalances by rewriting the histories through both practical and theoretical work. British-based artists, writers, and photographers have striven to reveal the partial and the partisan historical accounts of the past. Black women's critique of history has not only been on the level of pointing out and coming to terms with absences, but also through the expression of outrage about the ways in which we have been made visible, when history has chosen to acknowledge our existence. Of particular importance is the way in which European history has constructed our sexuality and our femininity, characterising us as deviating from those so-called feminine qualities which have been attributed to White European women. It should be remembered that such matters are not peripheral, but affect the way in which we regard and interact with each other on a daily basis in the social and political sphere.

Women and men of colour have frequently been defined in less than human terms by Europeans. Contemporary Black practitioners – painters, photographers, authors, film makers, and so on – having identified the oppressor's language for what it is, use, control and expand the vocabulary to create something that speaks to their own experiences. These acts of cultural enrichment and critical reassessment are a consistent feature of Black cultural practice and criticism: what is at stake is the recasting of conceptual frameworks in terms of 'race' and the historical determinants of the relationship between Black and White.

Whatever the temporal and cultural specificity of individual Black texts as varied as Toni Morrison's novels, Sonia Boyce's works of art, Ingrid Pollard's photographic work, Spike Lee's or Isaac Julien's films, their narratives and images correspond to current national and international issues and historical problems relating to 'race'. The texts produced by Black cultural workers constitute a crucial intervention in the debates about identity.

However, the use of the term 'Black' as an organising political strategy has become increasingly contentious. 'Black' is more and more difficult to locate and the use of generic terms such as 'ethnic minorities' has resulted in a number of problems, not least because such terms are unable to gloss over the fissures and disputes and differences within Black communities. Whilst it may be recognised on an intellectual level that organising around the notion of 'Blackness' is not enough to cohere across difference on a permanent basis, it is still seen as a necessary survival tactic. The characterisation of identities as fluid and of the power of binary oppositions as diminishing in theoretical discussions, does not necessarily correspond to the feelings and lived experiences of Black people in hostile societies. There are a multiplicity of strategies emerging to give expression to the contradictions and dilemmas involved in current cultural practice and the problematised relationship with various colonial histories. These still depend on a set of common, identifiable needs: I suspect that this will be the case for some time to come, even though the dependability of 'race' or gender or class as points of connection cannot be taken as given.

I have indicated that identity politics still are established with those engaged in the arts in the public/non-commercial sector and shape the way they see their practices. We have argued for a long, long time for Black artists to have access to sufficient financial resources for numerous activities: to obtain appropriate buildings: centrally placed, properly funded and with resourced archives of Black history and culture. This is seen as a way of consolidating the work that both contemporary artists and their forbears have carried out, embedding it in the national cultural consciousness.

In discussing history and colonial discourse and the racism inherent in those systems, the way in which such histories are enacted in the policies and practices of contemporary racism has to be recognised and contested. The representational forms, the media, and cultural and educational practices which are derived from and underpinned by those systems need to be exposed and subjected to close analysis.

One much contested practice is that of multiculturalism, a term usually invoked by institutions to cover a range of policies and practices which are supposedly designed to meet the needs of Black people often referred to as 'ethnic' and/or minorities. Historically, in Britain, it has been demonstrated that the designation of cultural producers and artists as 'Black', 'ethnic' and 'other' in institutions affects the way in which Black culture is perceived and how the parameters are set for its operation. The sad fact is that should 'multiculturalism' cease to exist, there is no evidence to suggest that there would be a corresponding rise in the number of Black practitioners supported in the so-called mainstream. However, it may be argued that such policies and departments mask the extent of the problem, the lack of real progress made, and act as a salve to guilty consciences.

Certainly, there is no conscious attempt to deal systematically with the specific problems related to class and gender under the rubric of

50

multiculturalism; it is a linear analysis of inequality. The important point is that compensatory schemes such as multicultural departments are only tenable – if at all – as a temporary measure. If organisations, institutions and funding agencies would stop impeding us in the first place, such departments could be dispensed with. This compensatory multiculturalism underpins the setting up of separate funds for Black and White organisations in a number of institutions which should not be allowed to become an end in itself. There is a seemingly open-ended remit for this style of multiculturalism with little sense of how systematic discriminatory procedures can be eliminated: and that is the real issue.

Struggle against 'race', gender and class discrimination in the arts is part of a struggle about discrimination in general since it is the social and political environment which validates professional ideologies and work practices. Black people's activities and employment within the cultural sector and their representation on television and on film, in the academy and the art gallery, are related to the structure, ideology, and culture of those institutions. Such institutions do not function in a neutral cultural arena, somehow separate from the rest of society. The museum, the art gallery, the cinema and the university indicate the thoughts, practices and beliefs of those who control and wield power in them. Thus, if a society defines a given group as inferior or superfluous to requirements, it is unable to give recognition to individual or group achievements.

I know that there is a struggle going on: not only against the forces of political reaction but also internally: amongst people of colour, amongst artists, and why should this not be the case? We should not try to elide our differences in approach or priorities for the sake of a quiet life today: complexity, dissensus, and contradiction can flourish productively. Those tensions can be made productive: we here want, as I understand it, to discuss the future which necessarily entails addressing issues raised by the past. We are looking to feed into debates which will produce policies that can construct a creative and inspirational vision for arts, culture and diversity into the millennium.

Black cultural activists and critics should be supported in trying to chart and interrogate the transformations of identity that affect the migrant, the settler, those designated others, who leave her or his country of origin with the loss of mythologised connections or familiar references or cultural certainties, to live in a society where they have been inferiorised for centuries.

The problem may be posed in the terms of a dilemma, or set of contradictions to be negotiated. The invocation of a sense of group identity is not contingent upon a notion of static identity, a consistent and immutable idea of self and community identity. It may be deployed in order to raise questions about the possibilities and limits of pluralism in complex, culturally diverse societies and 'nations'.

Black cultural commentators need spaces for these critical voices in order to assist in the advancement of cultural forms and practices. For historically grounded cultural reasons, the work of Black cultural critics and practitioners frequently offers a different critical world-view from those of White critics. These critical perspectives contribute to the understanding of the world and relations within it and the accepted, naturalised versions of world history and events are called into question.

Arts and culture are institutionally inscribed with questions of power. Questions about who has the power to institutionalise reviewing practices, funding policies, the legitimation of the canon, such questions constitute the politics of art. The image of the creative, isolated individual as producer is one of the myths of Western European culture and bears little relation to the experience of a woman making photographs, bringing up children, and struggling with racism.

Whether discussions are framed around Black arts, cultural diversity or New Internationalism, it is those politics which we have to get to grips with, together with an understanding of how the politics of art and culture are articulated through and with the politics of everyday racism.

4   The Emperor's spectacles

Anthony Everitt

As the British Empire was gradually dismantled after the Second World War, the proconsuls and the District Commissioners, the tea planters and the traders in rubber came home to the sad little, grey little Britain of the years of austerity. The country was set to dwindle into a marine Ruritania. But then an extraordinary thing happened. A gift from the Third World to an undeserving member of the First. Peoples from the Caribbean, from Asia, and from Africa followed their former overlords on a great trek from South to North. Thousands of migrants came to live and work in Britain, joining those Black people who, though few in number, had lived there for many generations. In a word, the Empire imploded. The consequence is that my country contains representatives of most of the world's cultures within its boundaries. The arts, the cuisines, the religions are all here. It is a gift of incomparable and incomputable price – as generous of the donor as (I am sorry to say) it has often appeared unwelcome to the recipient. After a generation or so had passed, the visitors became settled communities. Home was no longer Gujarat or St Lucia or Uganda. It is Brixton, Leicester, Liverpool.

   In the past three or four hundred years, the arrival of an absolutist state (I refer to the Tudor and Stuart monarchies) followed by the slow growth of a nationalist, imperial democracy ('We don't want to fight, but by jingo if we do...'), contributed to a one-dimensional view of the nature of Englishness. But the twentieth century has seen a return to a society which is not so much a single culture as a 'culture of cultures' (to borrow a term of Professor Chris Mullard). We have become once again (but this time peacefully) a much invaded island.

   The process began with the arrival of the Jews in full flight from Russian and East European pogroms. Hitler and the installation of the Iron Curtain, saw new waves of immigration from the Continent. Exiles from the Ukraine, Poland, Latvia, and so forth, still survive and thrive. Decolonisation brought the first numerically significant influx of Black people. According to the latest figures, the percentage of British Asians and Afro-Caribbeans is more than five per cent. At the same time old linguistic and ethnic minorities have been stirring on the periphery. More and more people are Welsh speakers. A revival of Gaelic culture in Scotland is in full spate.

The Arts Council of Great Britain has taken steps to reflect this fissile trend in its own priorities for action. As far as the development of the arts is concerned, our approach rests on an idea of cultural diversity – or, to use a more traditional word, multiculturalism. Our recently published strategy *A Creative Future* says: 'Cultural diversity must be a practical reality, and one not restricted to the art of particular communities or cultural aesthetics.' All cultures have, or more accurately deserve to have, an equitable place in our spending programmes. Our aim is a celebration of harmonious difference. We discriminate in favour of nobody, but seek to ensure that no artist is discriminated against.

I have come to believe that this admirable policy is not so open as it may seem. Last week I attended a public rally at the Houses of Parliament in London, the purpose of which was to argue the case that Britain should renew its membership of UNESCO. Someone asked what benefits the British would bring to UNESCO (apart from its membership fee) in the event of rejoining. At this point, the distinguished English critic, teacher, and former UNESCO bureaucrat Richard Hoggart made a decisive intervention. As well as some putative British skills in the management of committees and pragmatic decision-making, Dr Hoggart said that we would bring, along with other Europeans, to an organisation which stands above all for the multiculural idea, the Western ethical values on which, after all, UNESCO was based at its inception in the forties. 'I do not believe in cultural relativism,' he said.

Now here the ship hits the reefs which lie just below the surface of the water. Perhaps multiculturalism is an idea invented by Europeans. It purports to offer equal access and opportunities for dissemination to all cultures, to be inspired by the injustice of centuries of Western domination and to reject the hegemony of White over Black (and Yellow, and Brown). It makes those who implement its aspirations feel good. We march alongside the oppressed. But, does a sense of cultural superiority underlie our even-handedness? Let me illustrate my meaning by telling some of the story of the Arts Council of Great Britain's work in the field of cultural diversity.

A report by Naseem Khan in 1976, called *The arts that Britain ignores: The arts of ethnic minorities in Britain*, prompted our collective conscience and, in the early eighties, the Arts Council asserted its commitment to what we then called 'ethnic minority arts'. In 1985, we reviewed the success with which we had

54

implemented the policy and discovered 'no discernible difference' in our spending programmes. So, disappointed, we set a financial target (four per cent of our total expenditure) and some progress was made.

To achieve our purposes, we cooperated with activists for what we called Black arts, the term which followed the quickly discredited 'ethnic minority arts'. As time passed, we were interested to realise that we did more business with the Afro-Caribbean than the Asian communities. Why should this have been?

There are a number of reasons. Many Afro-Caribbean British are working class and more heavily politicised. On the face of it, the Asian communities are less extrovertly political, more self-contained, and include a powerful and wealthy middle class. But none of these factors is crucial. The essential point could be seen as a religious one. During the slave trade the ancestors of today's Afro-Caribbean peoples were kidnapped from Africa and forcibly Europeanised or, more precisely, Christianised. The subsequent colonisation of British Africa reinforced the effect. A Black historian once described the process succinctly. 'In the beginning the African had the land and the European the Bible: it was not long before the African had the Bible and the European the land.'

The recovery of African roots is a crucial personal and political enterprise for many Black British citizens. Much contemporary African art is culturally autonomous. But the culturally dissonant fact has to be faced that many Black British artists are also, and irretrievably, operating within a European cultural (postreligious) mind-set. Here an issue of great difficulty arises. Where the Afro-Caribbean artist may vigorously dissent from the established way of things in the United Kingdom, and may adopt a separatist approach to cultural development, their counterparts from the Indian subcontinent and the Far East often offer work which derives from *absolutely* non-European traditions. The Asian is not a changeling. The countries of the East suffered imperialism differently; they were not enslaved and resisted in large measure the persuasions of the Christian missionary.

The Arts Council of Great Britain is seeking to redress the balance between Asian and Afro-Caribbean arts. It is interesting to consider what attracts the praise of the well-meaning, White multiculturalist. Here is an example: one of the great success stories in Britain of the last ten years has been that of an Asian drama company, Tara. Its rise to fame culminated at the Royal National Theatre in London, when it gave a version of Molière's *Tartuffe* transferred to an Asian setting. This production attracted the respect of Asian audiences – an endorsement which I welcome. But to the White theatre-goer, it seemed to be giving a comforting lesson in cultural self-criticism – for this *Tartuffe* in translation gave a clear negative to contemporary religious Asian fundamentalists, from a satirical rationalist perspective. In sum, it was a work which appeared to demonstrate an Asian artist's willingness to operate within a European context, to inhabit the common European house. Not surprisingly, the cultural establishment received it with applause.

What is far more difficult for cultural planners is the challenge of fundamentalism itself. We British are made deeply uneasy by the Salman Rushdie affair; our instinct is scornfully to reject the Iranian attack on rationalism, tolerance, and what we define as universal, humane values. Some strands in the Islamic approach to the arts and to culture more generally defined are antipathetic to our own post-Enlightenment 'fundamentalism'. We say to ourselves that some cultures are better than others. Well, ours, anyway. Multiculturalism is like an invitation a host issues to his or her guests; everyone is welcome to stay provided they obey the conventions of the house.

A year ago I had the privilege of looking at the world briefly as it might appear through Muslim eyes. I took part in a conference on the Islamic arts held in London. I witnessed a discontented, schismatic quarrel about authenticity. On the one hand, there was an Arabian princess – whose views seemed to be those of a Western liberal, of whom there was a plentiful supply. A discussion of funding needs took place – and carefully oblique comments about democracy in the Near East. A certain uncertainty was in the air. Thus, when an architectural historian gave a lecture on Turkish architecture, she told the story of an unappeased search for the authentic. Architects oscillated between an unconvincing Bauhaus-influenced modernism and a retreat into a vernacular as feebly derivative as the medieval tithe barns with which supermarket chains now deform British suburbs. A striking image from Bertolucci's film, «The Last Emperor» comes to mind. In the heart of the Forbidden City in Peking, surrounded by eunuch courtiers and the antique ceremonials of the Manchu dynasty, the last Chinese Emperor recognises that he is short-sighted. 'The Emperor needs spectacles,' he says to an English diplomat. 'Like Harold Lloyd.' A remarkable feature of the triumph of the West is its ubiquity – as well as its capacity to plagiarise. Spectacles being a Chinese invention.

And indeed how *is* authenticity to be asserted in a world mediated by

56

European discourses? The *linguas francas* of philosophy, of political theory, of scientific and technological advance are all Western and coincide with a Western economic hegemony. Whether we like it or not, Europe is the water in which we all swim. It is important to acknowledge that Dr Hoggart was speaking out of an understanding of the reality of things, not as a chauvinist.

In contradistinction to the Westernising Liberals, the spokesmen at the conference who spoke with passion, with felt intelligence, were those who proposed a wholesale refusal of European values. They stood for a separatist Islam, full of energy, anger and renewal. Their emphasis, I am bound to say, was as absolutist as the most colonial of Eurocentrists, but it rang with conviction.

Where does all this leave the cultural planner in France or Holland or Great Britain? Here are some options. One: we continue to pursue our multi-cultural programme aiming towards an integrated society with diverse components. It is what most of our politicians and their constituents seek. As I have tried to show, this tacitly rests on the assumption of the superiority of European culture. Two: we could change track, and encourage difference, separation. Let us subsidise the fundamentalists, and the monocultural rejectionists who disbelieve in the principles on which the provision of subsidy is in fact based. But is it possible for a European institution to adopt such a policy without bad faith?

Perhaps the only way forward is to clean up our act and to replace the implicit absolutism underpinning multiculturalism with the relativity of *inter*culturalism. But this is easier said than done. The Absolute dies hard. A new British project illustrates one modest way by which a full acknowledgement of difference could be achieved.

The Arts Council of Great Britain has established the Institute of New International Visual Arts (INIVA). Its aim is to create a value-free 'space' which is not European, African, or Asian, where visual artists from all cultures can exchange ideas freely. A clearing in the forest. Its founding document points to a 'New Internationalism [which] recognises that all peoples and all cultures today are part of the same world. The Institute of New International Visual Arts will (...) develop new ways of looking at contemporary visual arts and their histories throughout the world, and to broaden their framework beyond the narrow boundaries of prevailing Eurocentric debate.' The Institute, founded last year, is promoting its own exhibition, developing an education programme, and publishing research.

Does INIVA offer a particular example of a way out of the multicultural impasse? The outcome will very probably be dissent rather than agreement, fragmentation rather than integration. Warring absolutes may simply collide and recollide, to little advantage, but at least there is the promise of an *open* debate. We will all be hosts, rather than some of us guests expected to be on best behaviour. And so far as Britain is concerned, noisily but perhaps creatively, the idea of Empire can, at least, but at last, be exploded.

Workshop «Crossing boundaries»

5   The long march from 'Ethnic Arts' to 'New Internationalism'

Gavin Jantjes

There is a desire in Europe for political, economic, and cultural unity. The word 'Europe' is being conceptually stretched to describe a new cultural space which is filled with the actions, words, and achievements of people that supposedly have a common foundation.

As the borders opened in 1993, Europe has taken the first steps into a new reality of national interrelationship. The question of who is a member of this new European family and who is not hangs heavily in the air. Europe has opened a debate about its identity and has through it revealed some amazing self-truths. European progress toward this new, imagined identity has its metaphor in Marcel Duchamp's «The bride stripped bare by her bachelors even». In the passionate race to embrace the object of their desire, the action of stripping, i.e., the removal of the barriers on route to the goal, becomes an act of self-revelation and a disturbing discovery that the desired object is more than the imagined pleasure dream of the European male; that it is filled with the cultural mechanics of the twenty-first century and is adrift and free-floating in its relationship to authority.

The aphorism that any definition of the self must include a definition of the 'other' is an explosive subtext to Europe's concerns with its newness. In defining who and what is European, one has also to say who and what is not. Suddenly the comfort of the old, loose, and general definitions of European-ness, which avoided a clear description of the European self, has shrunk to become tight-fitting and precise. Claiming something as European in 1993 makes it feel awkward and uncomfortable. It has made politicians and cultural bureaucrats become uneasy and self-conscious as they shift position in the debate about identity. Every affirmation is qualified by a subterfuge of pat phrases and hollow promises.

Those on the political right want this tight fit to resemble the skin around a sausage. They desire the *Kulturwurst* definition of European culture, want its skin to be White and its contents impervious to contamination. Others desire a return to the loose-fitting comfort that allowed them to intellectualise a liberal internationalism which in the last eighty years denied the modernity of the other.

Contemporary arts and cultural policy in Europe has to take into account the shifting nature of the cultural, political, and economic environments. A starting point for an 'open' European communality could be the hybrid nature of its various national cultures. No European culture is ethnically pure. The debate on a new European identity will reveal cultural reciprocity, syncretism and hybridity to be the very stuff of cultural history. As one unravels the polarised arguments of cultural purity on the one hand, and liberal internationalism on the other, there emerges a maxim that all cultures are multicultural phenomena. Any new European cultural identity will be one perforated with the complex interweaving of cultural differences and similarities. (Hall, 1992)

One can begin to think of Europe not as a classical novel whose realities are stable and fixed, but as a collection of heterogeneous narratives, which together describe a new European position.

As the nations in Europe shape their cultural policy around the issue of cultural difference, they have to make choices about the direction such policy will take. The determining factors are the historical circumstances, the levels of knowledge, the desire to change, and the will to share. The route taken in England (for that is an example I can narrate with some authority) was from paternalistic dictate to a dialogue about sharing; from 'Ethnic Arts' to 'New Internationalism'.

Making cultural policy which leads to change is a slow, delicate, and cumbersome job. It is like turning a sailing ocean liner 180 degrees in bad weather, before it leaves the harbour. One is asking for great helmsmanship, patience, trust that the engines will deliver the power to complete the manoeuvre, and that all the passengers don't mutiny, or jump the ship in terror.

Let us look back just ten years at the situation in Britain. There was an active Black arts community.* There were cultural activists with leadership skills. There was abundant artistic production, some of it of a very high order. Yet none of this had a place in the mainstream of British cultural life. Very few artists were functioning as professionals, which means that all their income was earned from their creative talents within a particular artistic discipline. Most functioned as semi-professional and amateur artists, even though the latter term discredits the quality of their work.

It was clear that the systems of support given to the mainstream White British artist was not given to the art and artists in the other sector. It was not that the artists had refused or not sought support, the history of their struggle was twenty years old. They were simply being ignored by a system that had neglected its political duty to help them. Some of them had lived in Britain for more than twenty years. A large number of these artists were not immigrants, they were by birth citizens. Their parents paid taxes and what they produced as artists was technically speaking a part of the national culture, yet as a cultural product quite distinct and different. Here lay the initial problems, those of language and of definition.

The activists' battle with the establishment had forced the creation of a division of art subsidy called the 'Arts of Ethnic Minorities', or 'Ethnic Arts'. It was an appeasement, a laurel wreath, thrown to an angry Black constituency by a reluctant cultural establishment; an action to disclaim the charges of years of racist inactivity. The syntax and semantics of the discourses around 'ethnic arts' were clearly about denial. The denial of an identity, of opportunity, and, most damaging of all, the denial of modernity. The establishment had created a two-world structure. Them over there, and us over here. It institutionalised a binary system of oppositional or antagonised representations which inevitably accepted the dominant Western/Eurocentric position dictating the nature and terms of its relationship with otherness.

The definition of 'ethnic arts' was created by the mainstream that controlled what was to be done, who was to do it, with how much money, etc. It ventriloquised a voice for this sector and demanded gratitude. It spoke of these artists as immigrants, as outsiders, as foreigners, as guests. All definitions to separate the 'other' from the mainstream. This was not a democratic policy, it was just a continuation of disgusting and paternalistic

---

* The term 'Black' is used here to describe people of colour, those who suffer cultural discrimination, and those who have a cultural root different to the European mainstream.

colonial methodology.

It was also clear that the level of knowledge about the artists and about their achievements was shallow, and in part nonexistent. If change were to happen it would require extensive retraining of racist officers in the cultural institutions or their replacement with skilled and knowledgeable public servants. The institutions lacked representatives and advisors who could initiate and sustain a change in attitude about cultural difference from within. The system of cultural support itself had many facets and branches. It required an attitudinal shift in as many of them as possible if there were to be any hope of a new cultural position.

Art education in schools and academies was vital to the status quo. Questions of value, aesthetics, innovation, and history were built upon a volume of knowledge rooted in Western/Eurocentrism. Alternatives were needed and cultural policy had to assist in their construction. New audiences was another dimension of the system. The existing audience had to develop a pallet for the art they had been denied, in order that they could engage and support it as part of their national culture. There were the Black communities themselves who had to realise that, when the new work was presented, the fact that it related to their experiences and their attendance to it was a valuable cultural exchange worth spending time and money on.

The other realities Britain faced were the desire to change, and the need to share. It was clear that what needed changing was the national consciousness about the arts. Britain had to understand that it had become a multicultural society as a result of its own historical actions (colonialism) and the actions of others (immigration). Britain was a postmodern culture long before that term entered the artistic debate. The problem was that the British were educated to ignore this cultural reality; or to think of it as a fringe benefit of colonialism, rather than a change to the foundations of British national culture itself.

If one stood at Piccadilly Circus in London hungry for a meal, one could choose to eat anywhere in the world by walking no more than four hundred paces in any direction. The inner cities of Britain were microcosms of the world Britain had once colonised, and one could not traverse them without brushing up against this diversity. In the arena of sports and personalities, there were people who carried the British Banner to amazing victories and it was never a question that they were not part of the nation. If Black people could make distinctive contributions to the nation's sporting culture then why not to its artistic culture?

62

The myth of British culture being insular and racially specific was slowly crumbling under the evidence of cross-cultural mixing with both European and extra-European cultures. What had once been the periphery had come home to roost in the centre and the centre now had to change to contain a spontaneous internal combustion which had erupted in Brixton, Toxteth and Moss Side in the early eighties. Britain had to engage in a dialogue with the cultural other in its midst, in order to gain a perspective on the future. It had to construct policies which allowed that dialogue to develop into plans for action. It had also to accept the national culture as a heterogeneous and kinetic organism in which individuals and groups negotiate their positions and identities. The national culture no longer had one central tap root but had become rhizomatic[*]. (Deleuze and Guattari, 1991, p. 9).

The desire for change meant a re-assessment of the way national resources for the arts were being shared. One could not have the one without the other. One could not expect this new sector of the culturally diverse arts to survive with any great success if it was not properly funded. In a time of Thatcherite stringency, no new money was expected and it meant that the changes had to be made on existing budgets. A tough task, requiring of the nationally delegated institutions that they did their obligated duty as managers of artistic policy.

An assessment of the situation in Britain ten years ago made clear the need for policy changes that would have to work in conjunction with timetables for action. The policy had to generate a national debate about the need for change. It had to spell out the benefits to the nation resulting from the policy shift. The communities directly benefiting from the change had to feel that they were a part of the policy making decisions. They wanted their voice to be heard and hoped to register institutional support for that voice in the debates about change.

---

[*]   The authors have taken the principles of biological (plant) growth and applied it to
       philosophy. They set out six principles which outline the characterictics of a rhizome.
       (A rhizome is a rootstock, like a ginger root, that grows in a multiple growth system.)
       The key difference between the centred, or tap root logic, and rhizomatic logic is that the
       first is a trace of something that has fixed rules of growth, arising from a traditional core
       of knowledge, while the second is a form of map-making, a process of creative and novel
       description of knowledge as it arises. Applying this to cultural development, there are
       tap-rooted cultures and rhizomatic cultures. The first uses knowledge from a fixed or
       centred source, the second develops cultural knowledge through experimentation.

What all of this meant to an institution such as the Arts Council of Great Britain was the inclusion of the nation's diversity into all of its thought and actions. The advisory panels of the council were restructured and appropriate people appointed. The council itself improved its membership by admitting Black people to it and giving them not just the specific task of advising on cultural diversity but on all matters affecting arts subsidy and policy. In order that a clear and timetabled policy was created, the council set up a special committee to advise it on policy. It was given political authority, a working budget, and reported to the council on a regular basis about its findings. This meant that the question of cultural diversity was constantly on the top table of the nation's most important arts institution and that the debate was led from there.[*]

The organisations in receipt of council subsidy (those who took tax payers' money to make and present art) were asked to inform the council on how they intended to spend four per cent of their budgets on cultural diversity over a period of two years. These reports were assessed by the officers of the council, with support from advisers and the special committee, and where they found it lacking, the council offered help to the organisations in the form of advice and personnel. Specialists went into these organisations to work with them and help them develop their ideas on cultural diversity. No organisation was bullied into doing something it felt it could not do.

This meant that existing 'White' institutions were slowly moving to support Black artists but the council itself had to answer the question of how independent Black arts organisations were to receive direct and sustained support. In the forty years of the Arts Council creating arts venues in Britain – and by that one means buildings – none was for a Black or multicultural organisation. The fear of creating a cultural apartheid with separate and special institutions for Black or multicultural arts arose. The council decided to support Black organisations on the advice it received from the Black arts sector in the dialogue it had established with them. The council responded boldly to a recognised need and desire by Black people to set up and run their own organisations. It understood that these organisations aimed not to distance themselves from the mainstream but to install a working platform

---

[*]   The committee was known as the Monitoring Committee. It was set up in 1986 and published a final report of its findings *Toward cultural diversity* in 1988. This report was accepted by the Arts Council of Great Britain and became the framework for its policy on cultural diversity.

from which to launch their particular art forms into it.

What Black artists were saying at this juncture was that they were not confident that the mainstream institutions were going to deliver the opportunities they needed in order for them to make an impact on the national culture. They were talking from experience, for the history of the struggle for Black arts showed that, in the early sixties, at the time of the creation of the Commonwealth Institute in London, there was a keen interest in the arts of others. However this never developed into any programme for real change in the national culture. After a few attempts at presenting cultural difference, the vogue lost its momentum and the institutions returned to their old ways. The artists were left without the support structure to make that great leap forwards into the mainstream and sustain a presence there.

Cultural diversity and difference also pose a critical alternative to the supposed monopoly of truth the mainstream believes it has. It would be difficult to argue such a critical alternative in an arena where the rules and regulations were controlled by those who at times still believed in that monopoly of truth. The Arts Council's decision to support Black organisations was therefore an affirmation for the freedom of expression, and for the democratic rights of artists.

Opposition to the council's decision came from two quarters: those who saw no separatism in the previous years of Western/Eurocentric exclusivity, and thus no need for new organisations; and those who felt that the mainstream was being given an excuse not to perform according to the policy of cultural diversity. In short, that Black organisations were there to do their multicultural work for them.

The council took the latter criticism seriously. It was aware of the enormous difficulty of forcing its recipient organisations into supporting any policy willy nilly. It installed a system of controlled assessment of its clients' spending on cultural diversity. This would give a minimum assurance of support by all for the policy. Every client now has to publish its spending on cultural diversity.

As Britain goes into the new 'open' European nineties, it can look back at a fair level of success in terms of policy development around the issue of cultural diversity. It can point to examples of good practice, and to strategies of controlling and supporting equality in the future. However, the story of Britain's march is not over. Britain is not yet a multicultural haven free of racism. There is still much to be done to pilot this giant ship out of the harbour. The dynamics of postmodernism in the arts, the on-rushing millennium, have along with other factors become part of the kinetic process of change. Artists are affected by this dynamism and bring their own innovative and visionary sensibilities to it. The result has been a critical rethink in Britain of the whole question of diversity and the political and cultural strategies used to implement it.

In the visual arts for example, artists have moved from multiculturalism to the dynamic idea of New Internationalism. The Arts Council is helping to set up the Institute of New International Visual Arts, (INIVA), which will become an institution with four equal branches of activity. Research, exhibitions, publications, and education are departments to be housed in its building in central London. The concept of New Internationalism is inclusive as opposed to the exclusive, modernist internationalism of old. Its thesis is the contemporary work of artists from all over the world, with emphasis on the art neglected by art history because of race, gender, and cultural difference. Its task is not only to question but also to broaden our knowledge of art history and the practice of art today.

What this means in terms of policy is that the national culture is being placed in relationship to the global. The questions of Black arts and cultural diversity will be subsumed by the new position and will function in a more balanced and reciprocal relationship within it. The Arts Council is moving closer to Paul Ricoeur's observation that: 'When we discover that there are several cultures instead of just one and consequently at the time that we acknowledge the end of a sort of cultural monopoly, be it illusory or real, we are threatened with the destruction of our own discovery. Suddenly it becomes possible that there are just others, that we ourselves are an "other" among others.' (Ricoeur, 1965, p. 278)

Arriving at this point in its policy development has not been easy nor painless. Yet it is an example of openmindedness others in Europe will want to emulate. They may believe that it would now be possible to use the British example as a vaulting pole with which to jump over the middle ground between 'Ethnic Arts' and 'New Internationalism'. One can only advise against this, for there is no short cut to the generative dialogue each European state will have to seek with its diverse cultural constituencies. The British example is a map, nothing more; those who use it still have to walk the long and difficult road into the future.

Workshop «Crossing boundaries»

6 Art policy in a multicultural society

Report by Geke van der Wal

Delegates from the Netherlands, the United Kingdom, and France participated in this workshop, chaired by John Stringham. Questions raised during the session included: Is there such a thing as a national culture? Who makes up that culture? Why are artists of other ethnic origin excluded? Is there sufficient quality among 'ethnic' artists? Where and how does one find them? Which elements are fundamental to a multicultural art policy? What role should the arts councils play?

National culture

Gavin Jantjes, a South African painter now living in London who is active in British art policy, noticed when discussing cultural diversity with art bureaucrats that they take very clear positions on national culture. 'A German, they say, is someone who holds a German passport. That's it. When you want to be part of that national culture, the first criterion is are you recognised as a citizen. If not, then you can lay no claim to the national culture. Then you have a situation where there is a tolerance of another person's culture. Still, this tolerance is outside of the national culture! The question is what then are we going to do with the large "ethnic" communities, for example, in France, now that they have become a part of the mechanics of a national culture. Where do they fit? How do you make them fit? You can't do that if you're not prepared to change the national consciousness.'

In the sports arena, Jantjes continued, you had sportsmen and women, French or British citizens who came from Africa, from all over the world, and represented France or Britain. 'Now, why can't they also be part of the cultural arena? The policy should let that happen. If not, you will only be window dressing.'

Another participant of the workshop active in art policy in the United Kingdom was Peter Blackman. He is head of the department of cultural diversity of the Arts Council of Great Britain. He stressed that when speaking about the arts we should not forget that it was also a matter of human rights. 'We could just as well talk about housing, education, about medicine. We should not separate those things, they're all part of social engineering.' Peter Blackman told that in the Britain's art world the fear of ghettoisation had gone. 'We want to start an integrative process with everybody. We're busy with a Black art national network. We're proposing to work together with the regions in England to try to establish a kind of pan-European network in cultural diversity, based on action and active process. That, we hope, will give the artists a reason to come together, working as a European, obviously mixed, team.'

Rudi Kross raised his eyebrows and said doubtfully: 'Isn't that highly idealistic?' Kross is a Dutch writer, publicist, television editor and member of the Dutch Arts Council. He was interested in the work of the Arts Council of Great Britain, especially in its four percent budget policy, the percentage of the budget designated for multicultural arts. Was that successful? In the Dutch Arts Council, he explained, an opposite process seemed to be operating at present.

Gavin Jantjes offered to explain this policy. He recalled the time he arrived in Britain, in 1982. There was a huge struggle going on among artists who were extremely good but just could not get a foot between the door of the system. What was preventing that from happening? Jantjes – coming from Germany as an established painter, with an exhibition at one of the London galleries – wondered why it was possible for him to enter the art world and not for them. 'I realised that the mainstream galleries never showed any Black artists. And when you asked them why not, they simply said: "We don't know who they are!" When you asked: "Have you been looking?" they said: "We don't need to look, we've got so many artists, they are coming to us anyway." So there was no incentive on their part. But what they should do is go out, out of their own framework, in this case the framework of the galleries. They should go into communities, to artists who don't have support structures, to people who are working in their kitchens, in church halls, who are writing in public libraries. If they, the administrators of the art institutions, are not prepared to do that, then you are never going to get that change. If they are not doing that, then they are in my opinion not doing their public duty. Then they are bad at their job, and they should be replaced. That's what we did in Britain.'

Jantjes told that in 1982 the Arts Council had a collection of 16,000 pictures, bought from artists, which included only twelve pictures by Black artists. The collection, according to Jantjes, now has something like 6,000 pictures by Black artists. And the panel who compiles the collection is now in fact half Black and half White. Jantjes: 'They sit together and ask themselves: have we gone out to that little exhibition in Leicester? Previously, no, they hadn't, they only went to the mainstream galleries, which were not showing any Black artists.'

Double loyality

Driss El Yazami wanted to make some global remarks. He was the only workshop participant from France. Originally from Algeria, he now works in Paris as a journalist. He is also director of Génériques, an organization that specializes in the history and culture of migrants in France. Speaking about the different national traditions, he said. 'In the Netherlands or Britain you have pluralism, even when you are critical. In most of our home countries there is no pluralism. Our role is complicated, we are struggling with a double loyalty, or a non-loyalty. Lots of us assume a critical position towards Western culture. But at the same time, we have to have the same critical positions towards our culture of origin. I mention Salman Rushdie. You can't be silent about the human rights in your home country. Another problem is that in Europe you've got different communities living under different legal systems. A Moroccan in Holland can vote, a Moroccan in France can't. You can't have cultural development when people have no say in politics, when they have no equal rights.'

Acceptance and isolation

Some participants wished to know more about the situation in the Netherlands. What was the opposite process Rudi Kross spoke of? Atzo Nicolai, Secretary General of the Dutch Arts Council, explained that the council – unlike Britain's Arts Council – was only a advisory board. It is the Ministry which allocates the funds. Holland, Nicolai pointed out, had on the one hand a cultural tradition of acceptance; an acceptance of ethnic influences, of influences from abroad. A very good and strong tradition. On the other hand, it was noted for its sectarian system by which every religious or ethnic culture had its own system, fulfilled its own role in society, had its own niche and a bag of money and that was it. Acceptance and tolerance on the one hand, separatism and isolation on the other. 'In art policy circles,' Nicolai said, 'this tradition is under review. Until recent years, we had a special policy for ethnic cultures, for what we call the "minorities". We had a special amount of money and a commission who judged the requests for money and so on. Now we are veering more towards integration. Now we wonder if it wouldn't be better if we had members on the council itself who are specialised in the cultural arts of the minorities. At this moment, I must admit, we don't have enough ethnic members. And two years ago the special committee and procedure ceased to exist; if you want money for ethnic theatre, you have to apply to the theatre department like everyone else.'

Eltje Bos, who works at the Ministry of Welfare, Health and Cultural Affairs, added: 'One of the effects of the special budget for ethnic arts was that it made the regular organisations indifferent. They didn't feel obliged to pay them any attention any more. It had a we-and-them effect. That's why we decided to change it.'

Marco Bentz van den Berg, Secretary General of the Amsterdam Arts Council, explained that the situation in Amsterdam was much the same as in the rest of the country, except for certain specifics. 'We have three problems,' he said. 'First, there is an education problem. In Amsterdam 50 per cent of the school children are of ethnic origin. We give a high priority to education, including art education, because when you talk about multiculturalism and New Internationalism you should start with the children. So we focus on plans for more cultural education in schools. The second problem is the theatres. The Amsterdam theatres are funded by the city council, but concerning policy decisions there is no consultation whatsoever. They can do what they want. Of course, we can ask them to do something in order to attract new audiences, but they are under no obligation to do so. The third problem is one of quality. This year we received fourteen applications for grants. Only two got their money, because the other twelve were not good enough.'

The director of the Rotterdam Arts Council, Alle de Jonge, had the same experience. He reported that it was very hard to find representatives of ethnic groups to sit on the advisory boards. Development, according to De Jonge, was slow: 'Artistic quality is developing very slowly. We have to make enormous efforts to get anything out of the groups and artists. We have to keep them out of the quality discussions which are being conducted in other areas. It's rather like patronage, but we hope it will work.'

Jantjes was not convinced. He did not believe there could be such a lack of quality. He thought this had to do with the kind of support given to the mainstream and whether that support system was applicable to people who didn't belong to the mainstream. Lack of support is an important factor, he said. 'When artists do not have spaces to work in, if they do not have the time to create work, if they do not have the money to make new work, then of course you have a decline in quality. Also, if those artists don't get the chance to bump up to other quality experiences. How do you construct something like quality? How do you put it together? What we did in England was to take our very best Black actors and give them residencies within our national companies. We gave our very best dancers the opportunity to go abroad and to work with the best dancers in the world. We created for them the space, the possibilities and the money. That was a policy decision!'

De Jonge asked whether there were a lot of artists competing for the four per cent of the British Arts Council's budget. 'Yes, many,' Jantjes answered. 'And the quality varies from brilliant to garbage, to absolute rubbish.' But De Jonge maintained Holland was different. He believed there was a reason for the slow artistic development in the ethnic communities. 'The immigration strata in Holland differ from those in the UK. The immigration groups in Britain are much older, they've got different backgrounds. We've had groups coming in from Turkey and Morocco for the past twenty years. There were not many artists among these groups.'

Peter Blackman did not believe that. And he illustrated this with a short story. 'In 1977 we were looking for African dancers. When we made enquiries where to find them, we discovered that highly qualified African dancers who had come from Ghana were working sweeping the roads of London. We literally went around and found them in factories, making lights and bulbs. We found them amongst illegal immigrants. Now the core of the leading cultural dance group consists of people who in 1977 were sweeping the roads of London.'

Eltje Bos was not convinced, she agreed with De Jonge. 'The immigrants who came to Holland in the seventies were foreign workers who had no work in their own country. They were peasants, poor people, they didn't come from top ranks of their own society. For them is it very difficult to find a place in this society.'

John Schuster, researcher at Utrecht University, wondered whether they may have an infrastructure of which officials are unaware. In general, he

71

thought, too much attention was paid to the dichotomy between high and low culture, between the official and unofficial. 'We shouldn't split them like that, shouldn't freeze them in different scenes.'

'Right,' said Jantjes. A lot of the artists who were today functioning as 'high' artists had started off from very low positions. How did they become part of the national culture? Where did they get their support from? What enabled them to follow that route to this position? Indeed, support. And again, Jantjes underlined, you saw this difference. 'The one is seen as a part of the nation, and therefore needs to be supported, and the other one is not seen as part of the nation, and is therefore not or eventually preferentially supported. In the discussions about the money, the other part of the nation sits under the table picking the crumbs after the cake has been eaten. But they've got to be there, at the top table, feasting with you!'

Crossing boundaries

'It's all about crossing boundaries,' said John Schuster. 'It's a discussion about nations, about who belongs and who does not belong. The tendency is to reduce a nation to the biological essence. We should see it as an imaginary community that gives us the opportunity to break out of this prison of identities, to move out of polarities between us and them, between ethnic majority and ethnic minority. Don't see the migrant as a migrant, but as anybody, as somebody who contributes to the politics, to the culture. Don't fix people into identities.'

Everyone should be feasting at the table, but how should the money be allocated? The director of the Dutch National Performing Arts Fund, Henk Scholten, foresaw difficulties: 'Because some people are more equal than others. All of us have these ideas, but what do you do in practice when you have a limited amount of money. When a dance or theatre group asks for that money, you don't have enough. It's always like that. So you have to choose. And then you can choose between paternalistic, positive discrimination on the one hand, or the quality-is-quality-principle on the other. The result? The more equal win. And, to be honest, I don't know how to resolve these problems.'

Peter Blackman felt that the answer partly lay in the practical sphere. Ensure, he advised, that you have an adequate representation within the administration. The formula he always used was that the organisations at all levels should reflect the demographic profile of the general population. Not everyone agreed with Blackman's solution. Henk Scholten thought it overlooked social differences; all the White people on the advisory boards were from the upper echelons. What about women, someone else said. Or the handicapped, another added.

Blackman wanted to stress another point which had been slightly ignored in the discussion. 'The key issue is will White people be led by people from other cultures. Will they accept Black leadership, will they take their advice and instructions? We also have a class situation. Who runs companies, who manages them, who sits on boards? You have to train people. You can't expect someone who couldn't afford fish and chips yesterday to sit on a board tomorrow and manage a budget of 200,000 pounds. These are class issues.' That may be true, but did adequate representation solve the problem? No, one participant thought. Yes, another felt.

Liesbeth van Droffelaar, who works for the Utrecht City Council, sketched the function the council could fulfill in assessing works of art. 'The advisory committees are made up of people with Western backgrounds. If an artist with an Arabian background applies for a grant, how are we going to judge his or her work? We have no knowledge of the aesthetics of such countries. Much of that creative work receives no support because we can't assess it. In Utrecht we have one theatre, Rasa, that programmes non-Western performances. In other centres you find no theatre from India or dance from Pakistan because they know nothing about non-Western culture. So you have to broaden your knowledge, to find the people. And I'm sure they are out there.'

Yes, Gavin Jantjes agreed, and if you couldn't find them, you should go further down, go into art schools, to educational institutions. 'What did the Royal Ballet in the UK – whose entire cast exists of young, White girls and boys – do? They set up a programme for 600 young Black children from the age of six. In ten years time – the time it takes to produce a classical ballet dancer – a few of them will join the Royal Ballet. That is a positive policy step! It's development work. You have to spend a part of your budget on that – and control it. Because the Royal Opera House could say: Okay, we are prepared to spend four per cent of our budget, we will employ Jessye Norman for a season. Of course, that wouldn't do any good. They should say: we have a problem in our orchestra, not one of them is Black. And if they can't find them, they should go further down, to schools. There you will find a huge pool of kids interested in making music. All kinds of music. The reason that they mostly end up in rap and not in classical music has to do with support. We must change that, by policy decisions, by money, by incentives from the institutions, and from the Ministry.'

Workshop «Wider landscapes»

7   Defining qualities as opposed to quality

Tony van Dijk

Values, norms, perceptions and prejudices form the content of our consciousness and direct our actions. We think and act within a conceptual frame that is culturally determined. We think in one or more languages and express ourselves in language. We use language to communicate with one another. We use words for this and these reflect a specific organisation of the world as we see and experience it or as we would like to see it. Who and what we are depends on such factors as culture, environment, class, ethnicity, gender, upbringing, education, religion, and so forth. All these factors contribute to our cultural identity and make us who we are. They also influence our values and norms. Our frames of reference play a role not only in understanding the world but also in giving meaning to life.

Man is both creature and creator. On the one hand, he is a product of his culture; on the other, every individual creates his own culture and his own world, through his own interventions, by changing and renewing things. Man and his world are continuously evolving. It is not what this or any other culture has made of us that is important. What matters is what we ourselves do with this given, in our interaction with others, through reflection and introspection; what we try to make of ourselves, of our culture and our world. Each of us from his own standpoint.

We are not just conscious beings. We are endowed with self-consciousness. We normally regard 'self-consciousness' as a state. The question is whether we are also prepared to see self-consciousness as an activity which we can actively engage in. This demands effort, and it is precisely this philosophical and by no means everyday effort that we are asked to make when reflecting on how to define quality in the arts.

In order to arrive at a fruitful exchange of ideas, we first need to examine some of the central notions. This is necessary if the dialogue is to produce clear, realistic recommendations and interventions in the cultural and artistic sphere. This – that is, the formulation of recommendations for art policies in the nineties – is our task.

I shall examine two notions. First I shall explore the notions of 'art' and 'culture' in relation to universalism and relativism. Then I shall take a look at the significance of 'quality' and the judgement of quality in dealing with the arts in a multicultural society.

Art and culture / universalism and relativism

'Art' and 'culture' are concepts which have evolved within what we call Western culture. At some time in Western culture, people came to look upon 'culture' as a subject for reflection. The first attempts to elucidate what 'culture' is were undertaken by the ancient Greeks. Our concept of culture has been formed over the long intervening period, evolving via the Renaissance ideal of *homo universalis* and the full-fledged bourgeois society of the historicising nineteenth century.

The constitution and history of the notion of 'art' and the philosophical and theoretical considerations it has invoked are as rich as the history of art itself. The question is to what extent do these notions, so typical of Western culture, suffice when applied to the cultural expressions of other cultures or blends of cultures? A naive universalism, which is in fact Eurocentrism, would have us believe that there is only one concept of 'art' and only one goal or direction in which the development of every culture is moving. Western culture is the centre and vanguard, and our progress serves as a model for the rest of the world. However, cultural anthropology has shown that we need to extend the notion of culture. Culture embraces more than philosophy, art, science, religion, etc. Societal forms, political institutions, codes of behaviour, customs and traditions are intrinsic features which define a culture's unicity. The classical anthropologist sees every culture as hallmarked by its own system of values and norms which are valuable and fundamental to and directional for that community. Such values and norms are concretised in its products, significances and conventions.

The implication of this is that there is no Archimedean neutral point of view. There is no absolute cosmic criterion by which we can determine what is 'true' or what is a fundamental, so-called universal value. And so there is no universal norm. Everything is seemingly historically and culturally determined.

If we are critical, we will realise that universalism and relativism offer a

76

basis for tolerance and respect toward 'the other' on some occasions, while providing a premise for paternalism and superiority on others. Cultural relativism is no more capable than universalism of validating its own truth as the absolute truth. Since time immemorial cultures have influenced one another. By taming horses, pigeons, and so forth we have accelerated the speed at which we travel and communicate. Technology has multiplied and shortened our communication lines to a staggering degree. Our European societies have become multicultural. It is no wonder then that we are constantly required to question our conceptual frame as well as our values and norms and our tacit, implicit presuppositions. I see this as the moral duty of those who are key figures in the art world, who educate and stimulate artists; who assess and present their work.

We owe it to the arts and to ourselves to analyse the mechanisms we deploy to judge art and the context in which that judgement is made. The pluriformity of the arts today requires the development of a transcultural or multicultural frame when discussing form, colour, technique, content, expressivity, and quality.

Quality and the multicultural arts

In their search for a truly universal method of acquiring scientific knowledge of the world, philosophers have distinguished between primary and secondary properties. The primary properties are those which are measurable in some way and which can therefore be expressed in quantities. These can be objectively assessed. The secondary properties include subjective experiences such as smell, taste, which can be expressed in value judgements such as pleasant or unpleasant. Every time we contemplate art, or review a work of art, the exasperating question arises as to whether the quality of the object inheres in the object itself or whether it lies in the eye of the beholder.

The notion of quality has so many meanings and is so complex that it should be used with the utmost care. And even more so in the arts. For art embodies two aspects: on the one hand, it is judged on quality, on the other, art itself is the main source which generates and transforms the notion of quality in our culture. In 1991 the American art critic Thomas McEvilley gave a lecture at the Stedelijk Museum in Amsterdam. McEvilley claims there are countless indications that quality cannot be objectively defined and that it is not universal. Taste and views on taste are constantly subject to change.

77

Moreover, he points out that in different cultures in different parts of the world very different ideas on quality may be upheld at the same time. What may be considered a good painting or a good book by one group of art critics in Amsterdam, may well be judged less interesting by a group elsewhere.

According to McEvilley, 'quality, it seems, changes constantly both in regard to time and to place. The situation is not complete chaos, however. Quality judgements have a certain degree of stability within limited contexts of time and space. People in the same class, with the same education, in the same culture, at the same time in history, are apt to have similar ideas of quality, which means that their value judgements are meaningful among themselves.' The question then is whether in the nineties leeway will be granted for new and 'other' visions of quality.

Wider landscapes

As I said, man is both nature and culture; creature and creator. He is formed and in his turn forms. This involves a multitude of complex processes and mechanisms. In his celebrated work *Novum Organon*, the philosopher Francis Bacon (1561-1626) warns that we are all prone to deep fallacies of the mind by virtue of our human nature. Bacon, who became famous for the restoration of science and philosophy, lists in his *Novum Organon* four kinds of fallacies, or idols, as he calls them. The first category, the 'idols of the tribe', leads us to focus our attention on facts that confirm an attractive proposition and overlook others which refute it. The second, the 'idols of the cave', allude to the fact that every human being is deluded by personal prejudices, emotions, and passions. Thirdly, he mentions the 'idols of the market place', which are the fallacies caused by the inadequacy and deceptive nature of words. Lastly, he describes the 'idols of the theatre', which we take to refer to the social mechanisms involved when we express ourselves in the different roles we play. I mention our need to distinguish ourselves from others and stake out our territory, to curry favour and be valued by our fellow colleagues.

According to Bacon, it is necessary to purify the mind before we can approach the world with a fresh attitude and are capable of perceiving it in a new light. Being open and receptive to the qualities of 'the other' and the 'works of art of the other' is something which it is easier to pay lip-service to than to put into action. Nonetheless, I propose we resist the fallacies which Bacon warns us against in order to discover wider landscapes in the arts.

Workshop «Wider landscapes»

8 Defining quality in the arts

Report by Karen Gamester

Twelve representatives from France, Germany, the Netherlands, Switzerland, and the United Kingdom attended the workshop «Wider landscapes». Chaired by Ton Bevers, they faced the task of defining quality in the culturally diverse arts. In an attempt to come to grips with the subject, participants touched on a range of issues: the inadequacy of the Eurocentric vision, the need for a dialogue with other cultures, the impending breach of culture, non-aesthetic factors in the evaluation process, the tension between non-aesthetic and aesthetic criteria, the idea of permanent crisis and the borderline stance. A prominent role was assumed by the art historian Sarat Maharaj, who sought throughout the workshop to distil and structure the ideas thrown up by the discussions, which focused largely on the visual arts.

Erica Kubic, publicist and former curator at the Royal Tropical Institute's Children's Museum in Amsterdam, had just come back from the «College Art Conference» at Seattle which had been completely in the light of this issue. There they laid a responsibility to find qualities with the observers, with the critics, and art historians, not with the artists. She also noticed strong separatist tendencies and wondered how one could ever conceive a strategy that could reconcile an inclusive as well as an exclusive vision, although she saw some hope in Homi Bhabha's in-between stance, as expressed in chapter 1.

Eurocentrism

Chris Dercon, curator and director of Witte de With, Center for Contemporary Art in Rotterdam, warned that we should be careful of creating an inclusive genre that embraced all art. 'In order to be inclusive one first has to be exclusive.' He felt the problem was more urgent in the visual arts than in film, literature and architecture. He was opposed to the idea of the contemporary art museum consciously pursuing a policy of diversity, since it should automatically mirror new developments. 'We live in a culturally fragmented society and the endless fragmentation in the museums reflects the endless fragmentation in the contemporary arts themselves. I do programmes and the work of the Brazilian artist Helio Oiticica or the Chilean artist Eugenio Dittborn fits in perfectly precisely because I am an Eurocentric museum.'

Dercon's 'perverse' use of the word 'Eurocentric' provoked Sarat Maharaj to point out that he was appropriating the term in a differentiated sense. Originally from South Africa, Maharaj now lives in Britain where he lectures in art history and theory at Goldsmiths College, London. 'Eurocentric', he said, 'has eighteenth and nineteenth-century implications, and refers to a logic of looking which is dominating, which privileges itself and is racist and superiorising.'

'Nothing in art is Eurocentric,' insisted Zafer Senocak, a Berlin-based poet, essayist from Turkish descent. Art, he felt, was derived from the artist's subjective background which was today very complex. Modern European art was – so far as literature was concerned – an open area. Mirjam Westen, curator at the Gemeentemuseum Arnhem agreed. She noticed that art, film and literature today showed a capacity to absorb new influences, accommodate antitheses and transcend boundaries.

Art draws on traditions which are in turn a fusion of many traditions from other cultures, as Sevil Özsariyildiz explained. A Turkish architect, she now teaches and researches technical design and computer science at the Faculty of Architecture at the Technical University in Delft. When she researched the origins of Islamic geometric patterns, she discovered that thousands of years ago people all over the world had been preoccupied with these patterns. 'In the 1230s, the Moors founded the very first engineering faculty at the university of Cordoba and five people from France came to learn these patterns and applied them in their cathedrals, including the cathedral of Chartres. This is tradition. You can't define it. But it is a Eurocentric fusion. Everything flows into this centre.'

'Which means the Eurocentric tradition is partly founded on non-European traditions,' Mirjam Westen added. 'Then why was I not taught that at art school?' 'There's nothing Eurocentric about the fact that the Chartres cathedral came into being based on knowledge acquired in Cordoba,' said Tony van Dijk, regional manager for Holland's Open University. He studied cultural philosophy and aesthetics and is a member of the Dutch Arts Council. Van Dijk made a distinction between the history of art with its cross influences and art history, which is the account of that history. 'What is Eurocentric is if you write a history of the cathedral of Chartres and then you ignore that fact. The notion of art in museums is not Eurocentristic, I would simply say it's European.'

The modern art museum and contemporary art institute were set up, Chris Dercon explained, to provide a platform for art which no longer had a place in the Eurocentric Salons and art institutions of the nineteenth century and were based on the principle that good or bad art did not exist, merely art. Our attitude to art and the way we perceive art is largely conditioned by the art institutions, according to Tony van Dijk: 'The idea of independent, autonomous art is European. In the subculture of art, you have those who produce art, and those who receive it. In between you have the critics who are trained listeners who act as a guide to the less trained public, drawing things to your attention. Then you have the platforms where it is shown and people decide what is to be shown and what not. You have the arts councils who decide who is going to get the money and who is not. So it is the discourse, the exchange of ideas between these people and their interdependencies which determine our view. They all pretend that they have this pure position but of course it is impossible to achieve that state.'

The institutions, publicist and lecturer at the University of Utrecht Adi Martis told, have always played an influential role in determining what was art. 'Ignored by his own age, Duchamp owes his reputation to the American art of the forties, fifties, and sixties. It was not until the fifties and sixties in the States that Duchamp was discovered and promoted, in shows and exhibitions.' But Martis believed the museum of modern art had now become a closed institution like the Salons they replaced last century.

Chris Dercon was of the same opinion. They had to adapt again to accommodate the changes produced by multiculturalism. 'Again we are in the situation of the upheaval of art and of going beyond the genre of the unfinished and the finished painting. There is a new genre coming into being and the museum of modern art must once again stand open to art instead of attempting to define what is good and what is bad.' And Mirjam Westen maintained that, given the artist's dependency upon the institutional platform, the institutions had a responsibility to broaden their outlook and extend their frames of reference, in order to recognise and comprehend other cultural contents and contexts.

Need for dialogue

The problem becomes more complex when the ethnocentric view is fused with other ethnocentric influences, as Paolo Bianchi, an Italian-Swiss cultural critic, publicist and curator, commented: 'The problems arise when an artist from say Africa, taught by say Beuys, comes to Europe and seeks a suitable platform. He fits into neither the ethnological museum nor the modern art museum. At the modern art museum when they hear he is from Togo they send him to the Royal Tropical Institute and at the Royal Tropical Institute they say he isn't primitive enough and send him to the museum of modern art. Picasso and Cubism, for example, was a European invention and we created 'culture'. And the other cultures which we call tribes we considered to be 'nature'. It is difficult to continue to make this distinction nowadays because of migration. We are confronted in our own environment with this so-called primitive influx. Therefore, I am convinced the museum has to change its policy, its values of selection, and that this is only possible if we communicate more strongly with people from these other places – Latin America, Asia, Africa.'

Erica Kubic saw the prospect of being able to know these works of other cultures as the great adventure awaiting modern art institutions today – as in medieval times and the Renaissance. She believed mediators from other cultures – provided they were competent – could play a key role in providing such information. And help us gain access to these spaces in between, Mirjam Westen added. But even with such knowledge, Kubic continued, the observer – curator, critic, or public – could still only approach art from his or her own subjective historically and culturally determined perspective.

Breach of culture

Paolo Bianchi was also convinced that the present migration and intercultural dialogue would cause a breach in our modernist culture within the next two decades. 'The Euro-American culture will change. Our museums are a European construction. We can't look upon the museum as our own, like the Belgian museum director Jan Hoet who went to Africa and said there was no art in Africa. That is arrogant, though correct if viewed from a European standpoint. Africans have museums too and we should look and see how the African has adapted it and uses it to deal with his problems. Art, as we see it, is a European invention. If an African artist works with European materials we dismiss him by saying we do it better.'

Chris Dercon agreed: 'I refute Jan Hoet's words, there is art in Africa, but not the kind modernity has preached. Today we are on the breach of Eurocentrism. And precisely because we are on the breach we can sense it. And we sense that modernity is a completely confused programme and that we have to go back to a kind of pre-modern programme. Paolo uses in his writings the word "retrovision" - that is, the future is the past.'

Dercon thought we had to accept this constant fragmentation and see our programmes as a whole of singularities, adding: 'We can only constitute with the new data a programme in retrospect based on all these different kinds of singularities, where art or non-art from Africa fits in, Mallarmé and Renee Green fit in, outsiders like Paolo fit in, and the Eurovision of Duchamp fits in.'

Surely singularities necessitated making choices, commented Ria Lavrijsen, researcher and manager of the conference project, and that meant he would still be part of the system. 'But good art is not part of the system,' Zafer Senocak responded. 'It is impossible to make a universal health programme for all artists. As an artist I need exclusion. Without exclusion there is no art.' He was more concerned with finding a way of looking at the origins of art. 'It is always the same, we start talking about art and then we end up discussing the institutions. Maybe it is very difficult to find the right language to speak about art.'

Leonie See also used a different, spiritualistic vocabulary. She has a background in theatre and art history and currently conceptualises exhibitions and theatre projects as well as writing for art magazines as a cultural critic. Like Senocak, she too was concerned with other issues. The essential question for her was what inspired all art. 'I'm interested in finding out what connects all art, not relativism, but when is art art and what it really manifests.'

Sarat Maharaj felt that we could not establish a direct encounter with people within the cultures. At the same time we should not underestimate the degree to which the critical evaluation in other cultures are mirror images of the criteria used in the metropoles. 'We cannot be totally negative about what we call the Eurocentric tradition. Its big contribution is that it has created the climate under which we might raise and construct the issues of multi-culturalism. It has created the society of the museum, it has created the logic of the collectability, the logic of collecting, which is the Eurocentric logic, the logic of perceiving and looking, and becoming reflective about it. Those are the contributions of the European centre, and in this we find an alternative for the term Eurocentric. It is on that basis that the whole journey into the "other" begins and the shock of finding that the other might not always be exclusively the other but in fact can be a mimicking of the voice from the centre as it were.'

These are the complexities we needed to bear in mind, he thought, when considering the notion of quality and value-making. Here we were back to the concepts presented by Homi Bhabha 'about the in-between stance and not privileging purity, vis-a-vis hybridity, privileging in fact hybridity against purity, because that would simply be substituting Black for White and White for Black. In that way, we don't move out of the boundary position which in fact is what we should be making the object.'

Defining quality

These words focused the discussion once more on the problem of defining quality in the arts. Quality, said Mirjam Westen, was not a fixed concept. It varied with the context, the institutions, and the administrators, and the diversity of opinions made it impossible to discuss or define. Certainly it was no longer valid to talk about a work in terms of good and bad.

However, as Tony van Dijk pointed out, we are able to discriminate between intrinsic aesthetic criteria and art extrinsic criteria such as sociological, political, art historical criteria. Also it was unclear on what other grounds, e.g., visual, sociological (connections, fashionability), artists were excluded. Certain extrinsic criteria such as gender (female artists), race, or domicile (local artists) which the institutions applied, in pursuance of preferential policies, when selecting work clearly had nothing to do with quality in Mirjam Westen's experience, and were severely criticised in the Netherlands. And although she acknowledged the need to be more open to other cultures and favoured art intrinsic criteria, she realised that you could not say that every culture, every singularity, had its own value. And this raised the question of which institutions determined which culture was better than the other.

Chris Dercon believed that the autonomy of the work of art should always be the starting point for quality judgements. 'A "good" work of art always makes me forget all the other works of art I have seen before.' All criteria, framework, values and principles dissolved because a new set of principles inspired by the presence of the work of art became valid.

Quality appeared to Paolo Bianchi not to be bound by time, place, or to be subject to evolution: 'While the idea of technological progress and evolution is apparent in the things we produce, whose efficiency can be compared with the products of other countries, I'm convinced that the idea of progress is absent in culture and art. When you compare cave paintings in Algeria or Tanzania with new developments in art and culture they prove of comparable importance. This means that if an illiterate African tells us a story, his story or oral poetry or philosophy is not of a lower level that the story of an academic, and that computer graphics can be of the same quality as painting on canvas.' He was interested in establishing transcultural communication on this basis.

'You are talking about quality,' said Karim Traïdia, a film director of Algerian descent who is based in the Netherlands, 'but first you have to have a product to judge. The minority needs a chance to convert its potential.' He had heard someone say about film that the so-called 'minority cultures' were seen as a source of inspiration, but he wanted equal opportunity to achieve universality. 'There is a potential but not everyone in fact has the same chances. The range of choices open to the artist varies from person to person. Two people might ask, "What do we have to eat tonight?" The one has a whole variety to choose from while the other, say in Africa, might have nothing. For the minority it is imperative that we are given the chance to participate in this discussion about quality.'

Traïdia was keen to see a greater diversity of quality and richness of expression in the Netherlands. He thought this could be achieved if migrant artists were not only expected to be engaged with issues concerning their own community, and were given the opportunity to comment on Dutch life. But Adi Martis thought that diversity of quality undermined the idea of quality: 'It's nonsense to say high and low art are the same, that a Rembrandt is the same as a comic.' In his opinion quality implied exclusion.

Non-aesthetic criteria

Chris Dercon felt a need to go beyond the aesthetic view of defining quality and wanted to introduce a non-aesthetic component. 'Unlike architecture and film, the visual arts generate qualities themselves – they are the autogenesis of quality themselves. It is this in the face of multiculturalism which makes us renew our ideas.'

For Dercon one of the main issues was to establish when (under what conditions) is there quality, when is there art – and, later, when is there image? 'With these floatings of identity, of quality, and dynamic of quality, the main advantage of the creation of the Institute of New International Visual Arts in London[*] is that this issue can be raised there. This is a very important aesthetical criterion today.'

What makes it difficult to judge other art, Mirjam Westen believed, is the difficulty in identifying the context and content in other art, since it refers to traditions that are unfamiliar to the viewer. But judging such objective qualities as form, colour and technique would present no problem, maintained Tony van Dijk. 'Difficulties arise when the work enters into a dialogue, for instance, when it reinterprets earlier or other expressions. You need to know the frame of reference to understand these references to these other contexts. And this knowledge could be provided by mediators.'

Sarat Maharaj quoted what he called the classic example of the abstract expressionists themselves: 'Jackson Pollock's involvement with Zen calligraphy through to someone like Jasper Johns' work, which is seen as purely autonomous, abstract art, until one looks at the sources of Jasper Johns' work and discovers they are all medieval Indian paintings from tantric art. One would have to engage then with the dialogue on death that he opens in what looked like abstract paintings but which we cannot understand in the pure terms of self-genesis.'

The tension between aesthetic and non-aesthetic criteria

Sarat Maharaj did not think the autonomy of the values of criteria thrown up internally by the practice could resolve our understanding of Jasper Johns on their own. 'We suddenly bump into all those Indian sources and at that point we have to engage in the question of whether it is at all possible to leave out non-aesthetic, non-artistic factors that begin to demand attention in the value-making process. And in that value-making process in the late modern era, in the postmodern era, all these aesthetic, independent artistic criteria,

[*]   The Institute of New International Visual Arts (INIVA) was founded in London in 1991 to accommodate the concept of New Internationalism which places the work of non-European artists and those from minority cultures living in Western states alongside their American and European peers (see also Anthony Everitt, chapter 4).

may be in tension and in dialogue and fierce argument with the non-aesthetic, metaphysical, spiritual, sociological sets of factors.'

'We should take the great achievement of modernism,' he went on, 'which was the autonomy of aesthetic criteria, and then see it in this tense relationship with the non-aesthetic, and then we should come back to that larger terrain which Sevil Özsariyildiz and Paolo Bianchi have drawn our attention to, and which we could easily miss if we are caught up purely in the self-reflective moment in the art gallery with the Jasper Johns and Jackson Pollocks. That's fine, to some extent that's a valid domain, of interpretation and response, but is it the *fullest* – not the best. And there is a drive for a fuller, a more nuanced, a more modulated response, leading outside the domain of that autonomy into those questions of the so-called non-aesthetic criteria, which really high modernism wanted to exclude and wipe out totally from any moment in the evaluation process.' It was the acknowledgement of this tension, Sarat Maharaj maintained, that made the evaluation process difficult in the late twentieth century; and this was how he thought the issue of quality would have to be raised in this dialogue between this aesthetic and non-aesthetic criteria.

'Yes, I absolutely agree,' said Tony van Dijk, 'then we would have the future in our rear-view mirror. The future in art has stepped down from this ivory tower and its self-mystifying principle, which has been fruitful for a couple of decades, that art is an autonomous thing and should not be judged by criteria outside itself because we have to accept that, at this point in time, we have to take the *rest* into account, unless we want to go on with this very feeble, non-full form of experience.'

We would no longer make linear judgements of aesthetics, Chris Dercon elaborated, but would break up essentially nineteenth century-based history and value judgements and put these back together again, always going further but constantly looking back. 'And this is in line with the idea of art being about art today,' Ton Bevers noted.

Permanent crisis, existential demands

'If we accept that concept of art as a permanent crisis,' Sarat Maharaj continued, embroidering on an idea Dercon had expressed, 'and see it as a critical activity in the sense that it puts into crisis all concepts of art with which we arrived at a new work of art; if we tie that to this tension between

87

intrinsic factors, purely aesthetic criteria, and all those demands of an aesthetic kind, which in the early modernist period we thought we had shaken off and got rid of, but which have all arrived back with a vengeance and have gathered in the metropolitan cities as dark immigrants and women and the sexual minorities asking such questions as: Why can't I judge this work in terms of my culture, my femininity, why can't I discuss this work in terms of my homosexuality? I think precisely that establishment of the non-aesthetic moment gives us some understanding perhaps of the idea of permanent crisis, and that we should take that on board as an element in the evaluation process in the search for quality.'

For Chris Dercon it was not enough to identify the differences and that state of permanent crisis. It was important to maintain that state and question when and how those differences came about. The exhibition practice of juxtaposing did just that. Works that were juxtaposed were permitted to generate their own qualities 'because you have to reflect those qualities in a mirror. That mirror is your mirror and it's always changing, it's a broken mirror.'

Since some quality criteria had to emerge, Sarat Maharaj proposed reconciling a part of the criteria of evaluation inspired by the broader ethics of culture (Karim Traïdia), by the spiritual demand (Leonie See) and the notion of lifestyle (Sevil Özsariyildiz) under the term 'existential'. He took up his Jasper Johns example again: 'What are we looking at? Are we looking at the autonomous abstract painting or at a work that is taking us through purely aesthetic criteria only at the very end treacherously to plunge us into thinking about the metaphysics of life and death as introduced by Indian art? Now that moment is a tussle, which we have described as permanent crisis. How deep that crisis is, and how big the search is for the fullest response, now maybe the word for that is existential. It must throw into crisis all these categories with which we exist. Some of us may resolve that moment with the Jasper Johns in terms of purely aesthetic criteria, while others might engage in the full existential permanent crisis, and may feel totally unhinged and muddled after the exhibition, and others might only be interested in looking at the Jasper Johns as a springboard to purely non-aesthetic issues.'

How could one say that any one of these preresponses was better than the other? 'We have to begin to see,' Maharaj went on, 'that all of those responses are ultimately inspired by that notion of permanent crisis that an important work of art throws upon the viewer and perhaps that is the specific quality of this issue of evaluation in the late twentieth century.'

The notion of permanent crisis was adopted as the focus of attempts by the workshop to summarise what it understood by evaluation and the process of defing quality in the arts in the late twentieth century. According to Ria Lavrijsen this tied in with Homi Bhabha's views on negation and in the opinion of Leonie See there was a link with borderline art. There was also agreement on the appropriateness of the term: the original Greek *krisis* embraced the idea of catastrophe and second chance (Leonie See) and, as a medical term, it meant a crucial turning point when the patient either died or recovered (Tony van Dijk). It also conveyed the idea of the untamability of art (Adi Martis).

The tussle on the borderline

The discussion had come full circle, back to Erica Kubic's opening question of what strategies should be developed to ensure the art institutions were permanently responsive to the changing climate. Tony van Dijk proposed a specialised cross-cultural training that would train people in art institutions to view art through different eyes. Chris Dercon, backed by Ria Lavrijsen, was confident that the institutions were already adjusting to multiculturalism and that this process would continue through the renegotiation of views at such events as these. Others, however were less optimistic. Mirjam Westen: 'I'm white. People of another colour say that not a damn thing is changing.' Erica Kubic: 'In the USA, they say they are multicultural. It is a token recognition.' Perhaps the best strategy might be to promote what is at stake, Chris Dercon suggested: 'I no longer promote definitions but I promote that question of when and how and keep things moving, keep things in a tussle.'

Sarat Maharaj summarised the main findings of the workshop as follows: 'The achievement of modernism was to establish the autonomy of artistic criteria. Independent artistic criteria exist and that is the way a great deal of art in Western art operates. I don't think we can just say that all that is rubbish. There is a dialogue opening up acknowledging the non-aesthetic criteria which had been discarded in the arrogant moments of high modernism, when it had seen itself as the only way of establishing things, and believed it could get rid of all that, but all of that has now resurfaced. The dialogue, and the tussle, the echo of Homi Bhabha's notion of that negotiation from the borderline, this opens up. So we have these purely autonomous criteria and the very moment we affirm the very autonomous criteria, we find we can't settle the issue and then we shuttle back into non-aesthetic domains. And as soon as we go down that road, that too is leading us further and further outward, and we shuttle back into the domain of the aesthetic criteria. And I think that is the echo of that two-way movement in which we are not privileging the European nor the non-European perspective.'

Workshop «New connections»

9 Finding tomorrow's audience today [*]

Helen Denniston

Two months ago, my father and I enjoyed a performance of Porgy and Bess at the Royal Opera House London. The seat prices for this production, which starred the great Jamaican baritone Willard White, were normally priced between eight and 103 pounds (up to Dfl 269, or Fr 786). My Jamaican-born father, a British resident since 1948, is now 80 years of age. The reason that we and thousands of senior citizens, community groups, and school students could enjoy the music of Gershwin was due to the generosity of the socialist millionaire Paul Hamlyn. Every year Paul Hamlyn subsidises several Covent Garden performances and education programmes to help Covent Garden change its audience, but more importantly, to bring the experience of opera and ballet to the poorer members of the population.

In the Europe of diverse cultures and – we presume – new audiences, cultural organisations, theatres, galleries, might find this model of responding to culturally diverse audiences attractive. Certainly, the economic barrier is one of the undisputed problems for arts centres. But this model does in no way guarantee new long-term participation. The title of this presentation assumes a political role, in an arts institution or centre of excellence, which does not exist in general; their so-called political neutrality is usually the reason why governments wish to fund the arts.

And the magnificent Hamlyn Programme, whilst bringing pleasure to many people, will have little impact on the artistic and audience development policy of Covent Garden at other times of the year.

The arts centre, or cultural department, will need to find other models for action, and ask a range of questions to prepare for new connections. If cultural

[*] The writer wishes to thank the following officers at the South Bank Centre, London for their time and encouragement: Mike McCart, Jenny Waldeman, Alison Rowe, Ian Grant, and Ghislane Tawadros.

diversity and racism are a fact in *today's* society, is the 'arts' audience of today consistently sealed off from these experiences? What is the meaning of a major Black theatrical work being presented in an international opera house which otherwise shows little interest in engaging with Black people and communities? Can a European cultural centre encourage and celebrate aesthetic transformation that, as Marcuse said, must reveal 'the essence of reality in its appearance: the repressed potentialities of man and nature'. The work of art, Marcuse believed, 're-presents reality whilst accusing it'. (Marcuse, 1979) It is impossible to separate the arts audience from a wider discussion on culture and power. Art centres and institutions can or cannot choose to explore 'repressed potentialities' in society. But if they choose to do so, the traditional aesthetic vocabulary and concepts must be modified and adapted to a more dynamic social role.

The word 'audience' must be used in a more specific way if the cultural organisation is to become a learning organisation and reflective of present and future realities. Who is the audience? Are they passive or active observers? What do they want from their cultural experience? Which sections of the population are they drawn from? How can they engage and develop with the cultural experience of artists themselves?

Sadly, in Conservative Britain, a non-aesthetic vocabulary has been imparted to cultural organisations as well as education, social and health organisations. In the arts, the audience is customer or consumer: assumed to be shopping for the best bargains, the greatest choice; purchasers of services in what has been termed by an industrialist 'the social market'. Commercial sponsorship serves the audience member as a lover of dance, jazz, or music, and also as a potential insurance or banking customer.

But I feel strongly that audiences are partners in cultural communication and, as such, have an interest in accountability and responsiveness. To engage these audiences in cultural communication, the cultural organisation must use their skills and prestige, their cultural and symbolic capitals in a radically new way. It will have to regard marketing as one of its most effective tools of audience analysis. The marketing director of the South Bank recently quoted Theodor Levitt who states that effective marketing happens when an organisation succeeds to live in its customers' shoes, talk their language, think their thoughts, feel their emotions, and respond to their cues. (Levitt, 1986)

Cultural diversity means stepping into new shoes, new experiences. The cultural organisation must become a learning organisation, recognising its ability to directly describe social antagonisms, mysteries, oppressions, including racism, and recognising how far these are reflected in the actual cultural organisation concerning programming, employment, and audience development.

The Hamlyn Programme is an important tool as a start to reach new audiences, but the cultural organisation must begin a process of building accountability, responsiveness, and democracy which should permeate every aspect of their organisational culture. It is this model of a learning arts organisation that will be the most open to changes, 'new connections', and responding to 'repressed potentialities' in the society within which it operates.

The limits of cultural guardianship

The centres of excellence in our European cities carry the responsibility of cultural guardianship. The royal national theatres, national opera houses, the ballet and contemporary dance and visual art venues present – by European consent – the great achievements of Western European art, the great 'traditions' that contribute to national identity. These institutions should not be seen as separate from their small and medium-sized sister organisations. They and the academic art institutions, which authenticate the talents of new professionals, are part of a cultural ecosystem. In England there are clear cases of the subsidised music, film, and theatre sector acting as a research and development house for the commercial sector.

In terms of making new connections, where does the cultural organisation begin? It must look at where it is now, and where it wants to go. It must use both an inner eye, to examine its own organisation, and an outer eye to recognise its role and potential in the wider culture. In the wider society, of probably every European city, Black and cultural minority artists still struggle to engage with education and cultural production structures. They are undoubtedly marginalised and competing for scarce resources. The achievement of one centre must be seen against a continuing battle for space and recognition. There are additional battle grounds of representation and advocacy in key decision-making bodies and the major cultural industries.

The cultural organisation has the choice to engage with artists and their concerns, to assist in their progress, or to ignore the full cultural diversity within their midst, pretending that 'excellence' and 'aesthetics' are for the White European only.

The South Bank Centre, London

The South Bank Centre in London is one of the largest Arts Centres in Europe. The Royal Festival Hall, which seats 2,900 people, hosts the world's orchestras, conferences, jazz stars, and for three months of the year, the London Festival Ballet. Since 1987, the South Bank Centre Board has managed not only the Festival Hall, two smaller halls, a Craft Centre, but also the Hayward Gallery, an important contemporary visual art space.

Ten years ago, the quiet, comfortable character of this classical music venue was transformed by an aggressive interventionist cultural policy of a newly elected left-wing Greater London Council. The council, the municipal authority for London, was until 1983 a conservative body, permitting the Royal Festival Hall to function as a conventional orchestral garage. Pierre Boulez, a close friend of the current director Nicholas Snowman, remembers the old days: 'What happened before at the South Bank was an *hotel de passe*: a brothel where you hire a room for two hours and the proprietor closes his eyes and gives you the key, does its business and goes. And there is no artistic life. Just entertainment. I'm not against entertainment, but you must recognise it for what it is. You want your house full every night, you play Cats.' (White, 1992)

The cultural diversity at this time was Ravi Shankar, who had visited the Festival Hall since the late fifties, Frank Sinatra, and Russian folk dance spectaculars. Until 1981, the Royal Festival Hall was the only venue in which to enjoy one of the four London orchestras.

The Greater London Council's Arts and Recreation Committee seized the opportunity to democratise the South Bank. There were four strands to its policy: to increase access to the buildings, providing open foyers with free exhibitions, entertainment, and a range of food outlets; to extend the user base across class, gender, race, and age; to establish an education department which prioritised education and community partnerships – supporting access between artists and patrons; and fourth, to establish a new marketing strategy starting with a hugely expanded mailing list, to reach beyond the traditional middle-class music patrons.

A small, dedicated team refined the marketing and access policies. The education department prioritised the principles of partnerships with education and community groups, encouraging artists and public together and promoting enjoyment and understanding of all arts, exhibitions, and special events at the South Bank. It also managed a gamelan, donated in 1989 by the Indonesian Embassy. It is used by schools, individuals, and professional musicians within London's classical orchestras. This increased interest in gamelan within the United Kingdom, and the particular role of the South Bank led to a spectacular festival in 1989 – «Island to Island» – celebrating the art, craft, music, and poetry of Indonesia. A highlight of the festival was the *Gamelan and Wayang Kulit*, an all night music and shadow puppetry event. This took place in the large ballroom area of the hall, a flexible exhibition and dance space.

The new artistic director Nicholas Snowman forged a policy of programming works of living composers in defiance of the concert hall convention of recycling old works. Snowman also saw the enormous potential of the two smaller halls, which until the mid-eighties hosted mainly chamber music, folk and occasionally pop music. These performance spaces, with new lighting and technical facilities, opened up possiblities for music theatre, contemporary dance, and innovative work. An important aspect of the audience development strategy in the late eighties was to collaborate with promoters and festival organisations. For several years dance and mime festivals, capital jazz, the *Contemporary Music Network*, the *Asian Music Network* have expanded the South Bank programme. The internal expertise in classical music programming is occasionally challenged by fusion programmes or ensembles, such as *Kronos Quartet* who are breaking conventional boundaries in music.

These halls have been the seed bed for the cross-art programming which reaches a wider audience than previous years. They have, more importantly, been the first platforms for Britain's burgeoning Asian and African-Caribbean dance, World Music, alternative comedy and cabaret.

The South Bank recognises the role of the audience, the artist, and their professional development. Ten years of getting to know each segment of their audience has produced a highly responsive cultural organisation which has the mechanisms to react to new collaborations, new ideas in many cultural spheres.

Moving on from the multicultural audit

The traditional multicultural approach pursued by funding organisations has been to address the small or medium-sized theatre or music group with questions such as: How many cultural diversity shows are organised? Which

95

minorities are represented on your Board of management? 'How many cultural minorities are employed? Which jobs do they occupy, cleaner, secretary or artistic director? Whilst this range of questions engage with labour and power, there is another range of questions such as: What are your strengths as a cultural organisation? Which sort of opportunities does your centre offer? Who is expected to respond?

Whilst affirmative action policies will for some time be necessary for a cultural department or municipal authorities, it is important to recognise the abilities and strengths within centres of excellence to address contemporary cultural diversity. This is not to say that moving from a known to an unknown style of programming and policy will be without pain, without defensive reactions. Furthermore, funding agencies must be realistic in understanding the positive and negative capabilities within an organisation, including artistic, technical, and marketing personnel who will not all embrace change. Indeed, policy change, especially related to race and culture, will act, as A. Sivanandan asserted, like a barium meal, revealing the flaws within an organisation. (Sivanandan, 1986)

The symbolic capital of a centre such as the Hayward Gallery, part of the South Bank complex, cannot be matched by any other Black or independent gallery in London. From December 1989 to February 1990, the Hayward Gallery presented «The Other Story» – a history of Afro-Asian artists in Britain from 1945 to 1985. Curated by Rasheed Araeen, the exhibition gave an account of the relationship over a 40-year period between the artists who came to Britain after the Second World War from Africa, Asia, and the Caribbean and the artistic mainstream here, especially 'modernism'.

«The Other Story», organised after a ten-year gestation period, opened a few months after the Paris exhibition «Les Magiciens de la Terre», the first global contemporary art exhibition at the Centre Georges Pompidou. It ran at the same time as «White on Black» in the Royal Tropical Institute in Amsterdam. No doubt, all exhibitions were the result of vigorous lobbying of cultural institutions, and they represent the reclamation of the space and cultural capital of influential institutions, by Black and cultural minority artists. Most importantly, they make the Black imagination visible and attempt to interpret race as a social construction.

Rasheed Araeen faced criticism from artists who did not wish to appear in a cultural diversity exhibition; other artists were opposed to the gallery as a symbol of bourgeois patronage; they judged the South Bank an ill-suited platform for Black expression. There was also complaint of the low-ratio work of women artists. However, the exhibition did provide the first historical perspective on African, Caribbean and Asian artists; it did stimulate discussion on 'Otherness' and focused upon modernism, which had never been done before. It also illustrated the presence of sculptors and visual artists of non-Western descent in Britain since the fifties and their participation in the global art world. The catalogue is a valuable resource in itself.

«Colour of Europe»

In July 1991 the «Colour of Europe» Festival brought more than 100 artists of colour to the South Bank. Increasing public debate on the Single Market (1992) was denying the multicultural element of Europe and we felt that this could be challenged and explored through a festival. The festival, involving the Literature, Crafts, Arts Projects departments, assisted in developing their own connections with Black artists.

Several artists made their London debuts at the festival: Germaine Acogny, a contemporary African dancer, and Arona N'Diaye, her drummer, received a Time Out Award for Dance. Arona, a master djembe player, son of DouDou N'Diaye Rose, made two return trips to work with the London Sinfonietta, a prestigious contemporary music ensemble. Koffi Kokko, a Benin artist living in Paris, was subsequenly invited to Oxford to work with Peter Badejo, a highly respected Nigerian dancer and choreographer. The All-Night Qawwali attracted a new Asian audience, hitherto unseen at the South Bank. The all-night event, with breakfast on the terraces overlooking the River Thames, has become a new tradition at this centre of excellence.

The South Bank Centre has made good progress in providing platforms for Black and culturally diverse dancers, painters, sculptors, musicians, poets, and has integrated them into the mainstream programme. Many of these initiatives have assisted in new Black audience development, although this appears to be a longer-term, more complex project. The South Bank also continues to promote visual arts, poetry, and music projects which critically appraise the basis of its own cultural heritage; it is, thus, open to learning and changing. Its structure in terms of management and positions of influence is still predominantly White British and perhaps when their present re-structuring is complete they will discuss the priority of equal opportunity employment beyond artists and education tutors. There is still an acute shortage of Black and Asian administrators, directors, publicists, and technicians.

The funding agencies should celebrate the knowledge and skills of the South Bank and similar centres of excellence and assist them in developing these skills in the artists and audiences of tomorrow. Perhaps the experiences of the last ten years may be of use to sister European cultural organisations who are open and ready to change.

Workshop «New connections»

10 New participation:
Finding tomorrow's audience today

Report by Agnes Joseph

The workshop «New connections: Finding tomorrow's audience today» was chaired by Rik van Hulst, director of Arnhem's Schouwburg theatre, who invited Helen Denniston to summarise the issues she felt to be most crucial to the workshop theme. She mentions three points: 'First of all, we have to be very clear about the wider social role of arts and cultural development. We should look critically to see who is benefitting from the arts. Secondly, we have to identify our present and future audiences and ask ourselves what sort of relationships we want to establish with those audiences. How can we ensure that our art institutions, galleries, theatres, and museums enter into creative dialogue and accountability with those audiences? Thirdly, I would like to find out if there are models for alternative policies and for funding practices that may be relevant for the Netherlands or for us in the United Kingdom.'

Huib Schippers, involved in many areas of World Music and education, wishes to know the impact of policy changes on the shifts in audiences and on the international operations of the organisations affected, for instance, the changes that took place at the South Bank Centre. Several of the changes, Helen Denniston explains, have been due to political pressure by the Greater London Council[*], which wanted to see a new audience other than the White, middle-class public from the rich suburbs. Another factor was the development of the 'product mix programme' which offered, for instance, classical music on one night and jazz on another. Audiences are linked to other forms of entertainment. Up-coming television and radio stars also bring

[*]   The Greater London Council was the municipal authority for the city of London, but it
   was abolished by the Conservative national government in 1986.

99

in new audiences. There is still segregation between old and new audiences but the main point is that a new audience is showing up. In some cases, the audiences do not want to mix. Theme festivals offer the possibility to experiment.

Training

Walter Tjon, director of Scarabes, introduces another policy element. New audiences mean new products and new distribution systems and education at all levels. He points out that there is a lack of culturally diverse art administrators. In organising conferences such as this, it is important to involve trainees. Lola Young adds that the British experience has been to insist or strongly suggest that trainees be taken on for just this type of event. That helps to build an infrastructure with experienced people who can go into the mainstream or build an infrastructure within Black groups.

June Givanni from the British Film Institute, which is linked to 38 regional cinemas in Britain, draws attention to the need for continuity once a new audience has been found. This raises the question of the programmers' need for information on the films being produced and where they are available. It also implies the need to train programmers. Another important aspect concerns the monitoring of programmes to see whether they are successful.

Oscar Wibaut, programmer in The Hague's Schouwburg, wonders whether the British and Dutch situations are not different. He feels that the movement towards cultural unity and integration is relatively new in Holland, whereas in Britain this may have started a long time ago. In Holland, most migrants arrived in the fifties and sixties so that a second and third generation has only recently arisen. Thus, a new hybrid culture with different roots and origins is only just beginning to emerge. John Leerdam distinguishes four aspects: education, distribution, programming, and the second and third generation. Audience education is very important regardless of whether it is Caucasian, Black, Turkish, or Moroccan. This is as important as training art administrators, theatres, and film institutes in cultural diversity. Concerning distribution, he believes that as we live in the age of communication where everything is done through the media, we should not forget the crucial role played by television. Programming for a culturally diverse audience does not necessarily imply presenting programmes for specific

100

cultural groupings. While Leerdam is for integration, he does not see anything wrong in programming an all-Black or all-Moroccan production. 'Why does it have to be intercultural or interracial?' There should be both so that they can develop and inspire each other. What is important here is that the quality of the performance is not compromised.

While acknowledging the emergence of the new culture, it is important to bear in mind that the second and third generations who have grown up in Europe have developed different tastes and expressions from their cultures than their parents. Role models for these generations can have a big influence.

Winston Kout ponders aloud whether one should consider as the potential new audience people from outside the respective countries political and geographical frontiers. Should one see Turks living in Germany or in Turkey as a potential audience. Should the people in Holland be the target or the whole of Europe?

Nora Roozemond has always been concerned with the question of education. What kind of education must you impart to enable people to choose? Should one not begin with the educators? How do we reach the educators and encourage them to get involved in art education with a sense of participation? Since education is the starting point, how do we educate the four-to-thirteen age group in order to expand their skills? For this, it is also important to look at what is happening outside the school system. How can parents and community centres be involved? It is vital to focus on the children born here when thinking of the new audiences.

Belonging

Manus Brinkman, working in the museum sector, points out that the trend throughout the world is towards some kind of identity. A survey has been conducted in Dutch museums to find out why people visited certain museums and exhibitions. Surprisingly, most people said it gave them a sense of identity irrespective of whether the museum was in the Province of Friesland or in the multicultural city of Amsterdam; it was the feeling of belonging which motivated their visit.

When thinking of broadening the audience, we must accept that art is something elitist. In Holland the elite is mainly White. However, it is possible to broaden this elite by incorporating other aspects of the multicultural society. At the same time, it is important that museums and theatres create an

101

atmosphere with which people can identify. You still have this stereotypical phenomenon that artists from Africa, for instance, have the opportunity of exhibiting at the Royal Tropical Institute but not – or seldom – in modern art museums. That may be one of the reasons why you do not see Black visitors in the museum of modern art. They cannot identify at all. It is not so much the government that needs to change but the cultural elite and the museum director. The latter needs to create an atmosphere with which people can identify.

Helen Denniston suggested bringing back the idea of venues working closely together and in dialogue with artists from the communities in order to implement culturally diverse programmes. Further, she stressed the need for institutions with similar views to cooperate and develop a strategy aimed at their connecting with artists and becoming meaningful institutions.
A dialogue involves more than just the audience.

Walter Tjon gives an example of the «Coloured Festival» in Holland which is subsidised for educational reasons. An analysis of the results of this event shows that 60 per cent of the performances were imported and only nine were local productions. Remarking on the Dutch situation, John Leerdam also comments that professionals not trained in the Netherlands are not recognised as professionals by their Dutch colleagues. In his opinion, the lack of culturally diverse professionals is a result of the few attending Dutch schools. Once again the need for role models is stressed to motivate the youth.

Representation and television

Trevor Phillips is invited to comment on the idea that television is not only an educational tool, it is also able to contribute to presenting and developing art forms. Trevor Phillips points out that his view may be controversial. As far as representation goes on television, he believes that for many years minorities were invisible. In the last twenty years, however, this has not been the case. Black people were heard and seen more often, though mainly in cases of crisis to do with criminality or rioting. That has been changing over the last five years. Today, it has become chic to be Black.

Trevor Phillips sees presenting, producing, and directing television programmes as a craft and not as an art. He feels that there are not as many Black people working in television as there might be. That, of course, has an impact on what is produced and how it is produced. In his opinion, this is not so much the result of ill-will but of lack of knowledge. There are also positive things going on, he stresses, particularly in drama. Mainstream drama has genuinely made an effort to engage particularly with Black experience in Britain. However, this is frequently depreciated or weakened by the fact that the real creative well springs not from Black people but from White people. But he feels, there is still quite a serious problem. 'Part of the absence of Black people in the media has to do with us being a rather young community and people not having gained the skills, but a lot of it has to do with people believing that we can't do it.'

In Phillips's view, television may play an important role in terms of attracting new young Black audiences. The difficulty, however, is that nowadays people have so many more options as to how to spend their leisure time that they are much more selective. You have to persuade them not just to come in but that what you have to offer them is more interesting, more valuable, and more useful than television or Nintendo or any other thing that they might be doing. 'You have to target audiences much more specifically than in the past. The whole idea of trying to attract a mixed, hybrid cultural audience is a complete waste of time because it doesn't work. Particularly useful in attracting young audiences are performers known to young audiences from television. Young people may come just to see them, but once they are there they may find they are interested in other events billed.'

Cas Smithuijsen agrees with Trevor Phillips on targetting specific audiences for specific programmes. But he adds: 'People are very aware of quality but they stick to their speciality. People used to switch from one art form to another in the old days – theatre, music, dance. Now they tend to stick to their speciality. Even worse, they don't go to listen to music, they go to string quartets and stick to string quartets all their life.' Cas Smithuijsen feels that the ethnic arts is also becoming a speciality. 'There may be a group of people who will be sticking to that.'

Helen Denniston tells that British experience has shown this tendency to be short-lived. She quotes the example of the Theatre Royal Stratford East which is situated in a traditionally working-class area in East London. 'They had a very astute connection with a TV comedy show and promoted a play that had three actors from the TV show. They took on tour a sort of cabaret which they put on in the conventional theatre and transformed their audience. They retained their White theatre audience, but brought in a new young sector of audience who suddenly began to trust the theatre. They had a continuing relationship that allowed that new contact to then change the programme. So every season in Stratford East, there are a few Black plays and they have really hung on to this youth audience. This has completely regenerated the theatre.' From the alternative programming came the production «Five Guys named Moe» which went to the West End, adds Trevor Phillips.

Rik van Hulst stresses that the element of trust is very important, loyalty is something instinctive. In his intervention, Huib Schippers stresses four important aspects. 'First, we need to make an incredible effort to educate young people in the schools as potential audiences in a multicultural society, which means acquainting them with the full range of possiblities. In the end, they are the ones who choose. Some people will go to string quartets, despite having been familiarised with non-Western music and dance. Schools and children are going to be one of our main target groups if we want to educate new audiences and reach them.' Secondly, Schippers feels there are two possible approaches. The first is changing the threatre programmes: half Western programmes, half non-Western and fusion programmes. The second may involve a change of tactics: it may be necessary to work on marketing to make a product desirable. 'The main reason why people go somewhere is because it is desirable. Trust and desirability. Here one should not underestimate the potential of contact with community centres and the impact of word-of-mouth publicity.'

Thirdly, Schippers mentions cooperation with institutions that are large, open-minded, and have the resources. 'Within the larger institutions, it is fairly simple to form a department of people who work on programming for specific groups or for specific subjects. And this has been the approach adopted by a number of organisations, including the Amsterdam Music School. The idea of the World Music School in a school where previously chiefly Western classical music was taught has been catching on all over Holland.' His fourth point is an idea already raised by Walter Tjon: the crucial role of training art administrators so that in the future they can assume top positions in such institutions.

Lola Young stresses that the achievements in Britain are the result of a long process, and that changes did not happen overnight. Philip Hedly, director of Theatre Royal Stratford East, had a long-term vision of what place that theatre would have in the community, which had a lot of fascist National Front activity. It wasn't an easy area to tackle. 'In terms of education, we have been through so many shifts in our thinking – from assimilation, integration, multiculturalism, antiracism to cultural diversity. And now what has happened is a massive regression as a result of the central government's national curriculum, which is intended to exclude whatever gains we have made. This may serve as a warning. People get scared by cultural diversity. They want to have fixed ideas about where they belong in history. This so-called postmodern experience is a very disorienting and alienating one for a lot of people, which makes them go back in time and think that it was all better before these horrible people came. The successes and achievements were also the result of a continuous struggle, for which the Black people provided the impetus. One of the things that went wrong with multiculturalism and education was that it wasn't really a Black initiative. There wasn't a true kind of emotional investment in the process and so it ended up being a very disillusioning experience for a lot of people involved in the field. The Black people being trained have to take the lead and work together with White people. Obviously, it doesn't work if one group of people is pitted against the other. Again, at the end of the day, there are a lot of people who feel threatened because there are limited jobs and limited amounts of money and it feels as if you are on the line. It's very important to resist that kind of polarisation or that kind of anxiety.'

Lola Young also comments on themes already mentioned, such as identification and mixed audiences. 'There are ways you can have mixed audiences. On the streets of North London young people are mixing because they have grown up in this situation, it isn't anything alien that has happened to them. But this does not guarantee anything in terms of mutual tolerance and understanding though it has the potential. Our children are growing up together and there is a lot of cross-identification. In fact, there is a lot of White youth identifying with Black youth. You can see that all the time in terms of style, music, and dance. Rap is the major example. These popular art forms were initially seen as absolutely marginal. Now they have a huge market and have become part of the mainstream, with people from all races participating in it. There is potential for mixed audiences and that kind of cross-identification which cuts across the kind of awful categories that we have been used to. All of this cannot be taken without a proper understanding and analysis of racism and power. How power works, how it is distributed and how people can be empowered and made able to participate in the process.'

June Givanni feels it all has to do with the framework of elitism. 'A lot of institutions are granted aid to promote aspects of non-commercial art. In the British Film Institute (BFI) there is always the contention whether it should be dealing with material of popular film culture or whether it should be using government finance to promote the art film which has far greater difficulty reaching audiences. People come continuously to us with the request for, say, programmes of popular Indian (Hindi) cinema. But the BFI is mainly involved with classical Indian cinema, which is another tradition. So Asian people organise independently their own little festival for which they cannot get finances. You get parallel structures to the 'official' government-aided structure.' June Givanni points out that we should not treat non-Western art forms as the expressions of monolithic cultures. Within their own mother countries people tend to be differentiated, and come from different class positions. 'We have not yet dealt with the full complexity of these issues in the United Kingdom.'

Recommendations

The demographic changes in the Netherlands and other European countries force governments to develop both short and long-term policies to do justice to the present culturally diverse communities; also to respond to rising racism and xenophobia now manifest in the Netherlands and surrounding European countries.

The conference recognises the vital role of the arts and culture in our present pluralist societies in providing a focus for identities at a national, regional and community level. Europe is a crucible of cultures. Arts policies must recognise this heterogeneity and the heterogeneity within each of the cultural communities resident in Europe. Any assessment of arts policy must acknowledge the inevitability of conflict and tension within the process of cultural production.

With this in mind, the conference formulated the following policy recommendations concerning education and the strengthening of cultural infrastructure.

Education and training

1.   A coherent programme for children and young people involving artists, art institutions, and art educators to prepare them for a positive role in a multicultural society.

2.   To make available to artists and educators skill-development and access-training to increase their abilities to contribute to mainstream cultural life in a multicultural society.

3.   To consider the potential of other media in heightening awareness and appreciation of cultural diversity in the arts.

Representation

To draw up effective strategies to ensure representation and empowerment of the diverse cultural communities at all levels of all cultural activity.

Production and programming

1.   Governments should ensure that their subsidies encourage cultural diverse programming in art institutions.
2.   Governments should establish a production fund (simular to the one in Dutch broadcasting (Stimuleringsfonds) to support innovation and experiments.
3.   Art productions should be promoted by providing structures for cooperation between artists and existing institutions and their resources.

Marketing and research

We recommend that research and analysis of present and potential audience needs should be conducted to enable cultural organisations to reach new audiences.

Monitoring and evaluation

Monitoring groups should be set up to check implementation, progress and development of the above recommendations.

Networking

The governments should facilitate cultural diverse networks to exchange information between artists and cultural institutions.

Amsterdam, 10 February 1993.

Bibliography

Ahmed, Akbar S., *Postmodernism and Islam*. Routledge, London, 1992.

Alkema, Hanny (ed.), *Een kleurend podium. Multiculturele kunst in Nederland*. Amsterdam, Nederlands Theater Instituut, 1988.

Balibar, Etienne, and Immanuel Wallerstein. *Race, nation, class. Ambiguous identities*. London, Verso, 1991.

Bevers, Ton, 'Cultuurspreiding en cultuuroverdracht in historisch perspectief'. In: *Met den tooverstaf van ware kunst*. Leiden, Martinus Nijhoff, 1990.

Bhabha, Homi K., 'At the limits'. *Artforum* no. 9 (1989), p. 12.

Bhabha, Homi K., *The location of culture*. Routledge, London, 1993. (forthcoming)

Bhabha, Homi K. (ed.), *Nation and narration*. Routledge, London, 1990.

Bhabha, Homi K., 'Simultaneous translation: Modernity and the International', speech during the conference «Expanding Internationalism», Venice, May 27-28, 1990.

Bleich, Anet en Geke van der Wal, *Grensgangers. Leven tussen twee culturen*. Baarn/Den Haag, Ambo/Novib, 1990.

Blok, Cor, *Over de beoordeling van werken van beeldende kunst*. Amsterdam, Stichting Fonds voor beeldende kunsten, vormgeving en bouwkunst, 1992.

Boon, James, 'Why museums make me sad'. In: Ivan Karp and Steven D. Lavine (eds.), *Exhibiting cultures: The poetics and politics of museum display*. Washington: Smithsonian Press, 1991.

Boulez, Pierre, in interview with Michael John White. *Classical music*, 28 October 1992.

Bourdieu, Pierre, *Opstellen over smaak, habitus en het veldbegrip. Gekozen door Dick Pels*. Amsterdam, Van Gennep, 1989.

Brah, Avtar, 'The question of the New Europe racism, nationalism, ethnicity, gender'. (To be published in) *Feminist Review*, issue no. 45, Autumn 1993.

Braidotti, Rosi, *Patterns of dissonance*. Cambridge, Polity Press, 1991.

Brett, Guy, *Through our own eyes. Popular art and modern history*. London, GMP Publishers, 1987.

Les Cahiers no. 9, April 1991.

Calvino, Italo, *Le città invisibili*. Torino, Einaudi, 1972.

Calvino, Italo, *Lezioni Americane*. Torino, Garzanti, 1988.

Chambers, Iain, *Border dialogues. Journeys in postmodernity*. London, Routledge, 1990.

Chatwin, Bruce, *The songlines*. London, Picador, 1988.

Childers, Mary and bell hooks, 'A conversation about race and class'. In: Hirsch, Marianne and Evelyn Fox Keller (eds.), *Conflicts in feminism*. New York, Routledge, 1990.

Christian, Barbara, *Black feminist criticism. Perspectives on Black women writers*. Ontario (Canada), Pergamon Press, 1985.

Cixous, Hélène and Catherine Clement, *La jeune née*. Paris, U.G.E., 1975.

Dabydeen, David, *Hogarth's Blacks. Images of Black in eighteenth century English art*. Manchester, Manchester University Press, 1987.

Davis, Angela Y., *Women, culture and politics*. New York, Random House, 1984.

Deleuze, Gilles, *Anti-Oedipe*. Paris, Minuit, 1974.

Deleuze, Gilles and Félix Guattari, *Nomadology: The war machine*. New York, Semiotexte, 1986.

Deleuze, Gilles and Félix Guattari, 'Rhizome-fragments'. In: *Rhizome, A European art exhibition*. The Hague, the Netherlands Office for Fine Arts and Haags Gemeentemuseum, 1991.

Dent, Gina (ed.), *Black popular culture. A project by Michelle Wallace*. Seattle, Dia Centre for the Arts, Bay Press, 1992.

Duin, Lieke van, and Noraly Beyer, *Stagedoor colloquium*. Amsterdam, Nederlands Theater Instituut, 1984.

Epskamp, Kees, and Rob Thoolen. *Verre podia naderbij. Educatief reizen of cultureel toerisme*. Den Haag, Centrum voor de Studie van het Onderwijs in Ontwikkelingslanden (CESO), 1991.

Fanon, Frantz, *Black skin, white masks*, London, Pluto, 1990.

Featherstone, Mike (ed.), *Global culture. Nationalism, globalization and modernity*. London, Sage Publications, 1990.

Ferguson, Russel, Martha Gever, Trinh T. Minh-ha, Cornel West (eds.), *Out there. Marginalization and contemporary cultures*. New York, the New Museum of Contemporary Art, 1990.

Finkelkraut, Alain, *De imaginaire jood* (Le juif imaginaire). Amsterdam, Contact, 1992.

Finkelkraut, Alain, *De ondergang van het denken* (La défaite de la pensée). Amsterdam, Contact, 1988.

Foucault, Michel, *Interviews and other writings 1977-1984*. Ed. by Lawrence D. Kritzman. London, Routledge, 1988.

Gilroy, Paul, *There ain't no Black in the Union Jack*. London, Hutchinson/Unwin Hyman, 1987.

Gomez-Pena, Guillermo, *American Theatre* vol. 8, no. 7 (October 1991).

Goudzand, Henna en Fré Meijer (eds.), *Contrapunten. Mythen in de kunst van vrouwen*. Amsterdam, Furie/In de Knipscheer, 1991.

Green, Renee, interviewed by Elizabeth Brown, from a catalogue published by Allen the Memorial Art Museum, Oberlin College, Ohio.

Green, Renee, 'Sites of genealogy'. In: *Out of site*. New York, Institute of Contemporary Art, Long Island City.

Guptara, Prahbu, *Black British literature. An annotated bibliography*. London, Dangaroo Press, 1986.

Haerdter, Michael, Peter Sauerbaum, Kurt Scharf, Olaf Schwencke, Beate Winkler (eds.), *Facetten des Fremden. Europa zwischen Nationalismus und Integration*. Berlin, Argon Verlag, 1992.

Hall, Stuart, *Het minimale zelf en andere opstellen*. Amsterdam, SUA, 1991.

Hall, Stuart, 'Our Mongrel selves'. (from Borderlines). *New Statesman*, Sept. 1992.

Hall, Stuart, 'What is this "Black" in Black popular culture?' In: G. Dent (ed.), *Black popular culture*. Seattle, Dia Center for the arts, Bay Press, 1992.

Hall, Stuart, David Held and Tony McGrew (eds.), *Modernity and his futures. Understanding modern societies*. Cambridge, Polity Press in Association with the Open University, 1992.

Haraway, Donna, *Simians, cyborgs and women*. London, Free Association books, 1990.

Heidegger, Martin, 'Building, dwelling, thinking'. In: *Poetry, language, thought*. New York, Harper and Row, 1971.

Hill, Gary, interview with Gianni Romano, 'Inasmuch as it is always already taking place'. p. 39.

hooks, bell, *Black looks: Race and representation*. London, Turnaround, 1992.

hooks, bell, *Yearning. Race, gender, and cultural politics*. London, Turnaround, 1991.

hooks, bell and Cornel West, *Breaking bread. Insurgent Black intellectual life*. Boston, South End Press, 1991.

Howell, John, *Laurie Anderson*. New York, Thunder's Mouth Press, 1992.

Ignatieff, Michael, *The needs of strangers*. London, Hogart Press, 1990.

Irigaray, Luce, *Ce sexe quie n'en est pas un*. Paris, Minuit, 1977.

Jameson, Frederic, 'Postmodernism, the cultural logic of late capitalism'. *New Left Review*, 1984.

Julien, Isaac, and Colin MacCabe. *Diary of a young soul rebel*. London, British
Film Institute, 1991.

Kabbani, Rana, *Europe's myths of Orient*. London, Pandora Press, 1988.

Karp, Ivan and Steven D. Lavine, *Exhibiting cultures. The poetics and politics of
museum display*. Washington, Smithsonian Press, 1991.

Khan, Naseem, *The arts that Britain ignores: The arts of ethnic minorities in
Britain*. 1976. (report)

Kristeva, Juli, *De vreemdeling in onszelf*. Amsterdam, Contact, 1991.

Lavrijsen, Ria, *Black theatre on the move. Een verkenning van het Engelse Black
Theatre*. Amsterdam, Nederlands Theater Instituut, 1990.

Levitt, T., *The marketing imagination*. Collier Mac., 1986.

Lippard, Lucy R., *Mixed blessings: New art in a multicultural America*. New
York, Pantheon Books, 1990.

Marcuse, Herbert, *The aesthetic dimension towards a critique of Marxist aesthetics*.
Macmillan Education, 1979.

Mercer, Kobena, 'Back to my routes'. *TEN 8*, vol. 2 (1992), no. 3, p. 38.

Morrison, Toni, *Playing in the dark. Whiteness and the literary imagination*.
London, Harvard University Press, 1992.

New Connections: Finding tomorrow's audience today, Report on the Fifth Annual
Congress of the International Society of Performing Arts Administrators,
Los Angeles, 18-21 June, 1991.

Owusu, Kwesi (ed.), *Storms of the heart. An anthology of Black arts and culture*.
London, Camden Press, 1988.

Owusu, Kwesi, *The struggle for Black arts in Britain*. London, Comedia
Publishing Group, 1986.

Papastergiadis, Nikos, 'The South in the North'. *Third Text*, no. 14, Spring
1991, p. 46.

Pinto, David, *Interculturele communicatie*. Houten, Bohn Stafleu Van Loghum,
1990.

Procee, H., *Over de grenzen van culturen. Voorbij universalisme en relativisme*.
Meppel, Boom, 1991.

Ramdas, Anil, *De papagaai, de stier en de klimmende bougainvillea*. Amsterdam,
de Bezige Bij, 1992.

Reijnierse, Wim, *Etnische theatermakers op de toneelmarkt*. Rotterdam, Stichting
Buitenlandse Werknemers Rijnmond, 1989.

Report of the independent enquiry into Greater London Arts, chaired by A.
Sivanandan, 24 March 1986.

Ricoeur, Paul, 'Universal civilisation and national cultures'. 1961. In: *'History and truth'*. transl. by C.A. Kelbley. Evanston Press, North Western University Press, 1965.

Rushdie, Salman, *Imaginary homelands. Essays and criticism 1981-1991*. London, Granta Books (Penguin), 1992.

Rutherford, Jonathan (ed.), *Identity, community, culture, difference*. London, Lawrence & Wishart, 1990.

Said, Edward W., *Culture & Imperialism*. London, Chatto & Windus, 1993.

Said, Edward W., *Orientalism*. London, Penguin Books, 1991.

Sanders, Stephan, *Connie Francis of de onschuld van Amerika*. Amsterdam, de Bezige Bij, 1992.

Sanders, Stephan, *Gemengde ervaring, gemengde gevoelens. De Rushdie-affaire; een besluit tot inmenging*. Amsterdam, de Balie, 1989.

Schipper, Mineke, *Homo Caudatus. Verbeelding en macht in de letteren*. Baarn, Ambo, 1989.

Schlesinger Jr., Arthur M., *The disuniting of America. Reflections on a multicultural society*. New York, Norton, 1992.

See, Leonie, *Ich weiss was ich will*. Berlin, Orlanda Frauenverlag, 1991.

Senocak, Zafer, *Atlas des tropischen Deutschland*. Berlin, Babel Verlag Hund & Toker, 1992.

Shayegan, Daryush, *Le regard mutilé. Schizophrénie culturelle: pays traditionnels face à la modernité*. Paris, Albin Michel, 1989.

Showalter, Elaine, 'Borderlines'. In: *Sexual anarchy: Gender and culture in the Fin de Siècle*. London, Bloomsbury, 1990.

Spender, Dale, *Women of ideas and what men have done to them*. London, Women's Press, 1982.

Spivak, Gayatri C., 'Reading the satanic verses'. *Third Text*, summer 1990, pp. 41-60.

Spivak, Gayatri C., *In other worlds*. New York, Methuen, 1987.

Steinberg, Stephen, *The ethnic myth. Race, ethnicity, and class in America*. Boston, Beacon Press, 1989.

Swaan, Abram de, *Het lied van de kosmopoliet*. Amsterdam, Meulenhoff, 1987.

Swaan, Abram de, *Perron Nederland*. Amsterdam, Meulenhoff, 1991.

Tennekes, J., *De onbekende dimensie. Over cultuur, cultuurverschillen en macht*. Leuven/Apeldoorn, Garant, 1990.

Walker, Alice, *In search of our mother's gardens*. London, Women's Press, 1984.

Wallace, Michele, *Black macho and the myth of the Superwoman*. London, Verso, 1990.

Wallace, Michele, *Invisibility blues. From pop to theory*. London, Verso, 1990.

Welsch, Wolfgang, *Ästhetisches Denken*. Stuttgart, Reclam, 1990.

West, Cornel, 'The new cultural politics of difference'. In: Russell Ferguson et al (eds.), *Out there: Marginalization and contemporary cultures*. New York, the New Museum of Contemporary Art, 1990.

Wetenschappelijke Raad voor het Regeringsbeleid, *Allochtonenbeleid*. 's-Gravenhage, SDU, 1989.

White, Robert Young, *Mythologies: Writing, history and the West*. London, Routledge, 1991.

Williams, David (ed.), *Peter Brook and the Mahabharatha. Critical Perspectives*. London, Routledge, 1991.

Witte de With, *The lectures 1991. Witte de With*. Rotterdam, Centre for Contemporary Art, 1991.

Wolf, Christa, *Cassandra. A novel and four essays*. London, Virago Press, 1984.

Woolf, Virginia, *Three Guineas*. London, Penguin, 1938.

Ybarra-Frausto, Tomas, 'Chicano movement/Chicano art'. In: Ivan Karp and Steven D. Lavine (eds.), *Exhibiting cultures: The poetics and politics of museum display*. Washington, Smithsonian Press, 1991.

List of authors and workshop participants

Homi K. Bhabha is Professor of Comparative Literature and Literary Theory at the University of Sussex (UK). He has become a spokesman for a new field of critical thought in culture and visual arts. His writings on colonialism, race and identity will be published in a collection of essays entitled *The Location of Culture* by Routledge in 1993.

Rosi Braidotti is Professor and head of Women's Studies in the Humanities at the University of Utrecht. She received her Ph.D in philosophy from the Sorbonne in 1981 with a dissertation on Foucault and Feminism. She is the author of *Patterns of Dissonance: A study of Women in Contemporary Philosophy*. She has also published extensively on feminist theory in collections such as *Between Feminism and Psychoanalysis* and journals such as *Differences, Gender studies, Hypatia, Women's Studies International Forum, DWF, Cahiers de Grif*. She co-ordinates an Erasmus exchange network for women's studies, with seven European partners.

Helen Denniston is a consultant and lecturer in cultural policy, arts management, and communications. She is also a singer. She has conducted a range of arts policy research for national funding agencies, which focus on good practice in equal opportunities. In 1991 she directed the «Colour of Europe» Festival for the South Bank Centre London. Her current projects include leading a research team on Black Cultural Industries in Europe for the Comedia consultancy.

Tony van Dijk, is regional manager for Noord-Holland for the Dutch Open University. He studied Cultural Philosophy and Aesthetics and is a member of the Dutch Arts Council.

Anthony Everitt, is Secretary General of the Arts Council of Great Britain.

Gavin Jantjes, born in Cape Town (South Africa), is a painter and print maker. He was educated at the Michaelis School for Fine Arts, University of Cape Town, and at the Hochschule für Bildende Kunste in Hamburg. He was a consultant for the High Commissioner for Refugees (UNHCR) in Geneva and an advisor to the Visiting Arts Unit of the British Council. He has served as a member of the East Midlands Regional Arts Association and was member of the Arts Council of Great Britain from 1986 to 1990. He chaired the Monitoring Committee of the Council's Actionprogramme for Minority Arts and wrote the report *Towards Cultural Diversity*. In 1992 he was the consultant for the Arts Council's INIVA project.

Ria Lavrijsen is a Dutch publicist, since 1988 working in research, journalism and broadcasting. She initiated and organised the conference «Cultural diversity in the arts», February 1993 and is the editor of this publication under the same title. She researched Black theatre in Britain. Her (Dutch) book on the same subject is entitled *Black theatre on the move* (1990).

Aad Nuis is a Dutch member of parliament for D'66 and is chairman of the Government Committee for Culture and the Arts.

Lola Young is a publicist who lectures at Middlesex Polytechnic, London. She is involved in a wide variety of cultural development work relating to Black and ethnic arts, and is researching cultural theory, film theory, and race. She is currently working on a doctoral thesis on *Black sexuality in post-war British cinema*.

Chairpersons and secretaries of the workshops

Trevor Phillips is the editor and presenter of discussion programmes for London Weekend Television and has an outstanding reputation in chairing public debates for LWT and BBC Television.
Ton Bevers is Professor of Cultural Studies at the Erasmus University in Rotterdam.
Karen Gamester works as a free-lance translator, among others, for the Holland Festival and for *Kunst- en Museumjournaal*.
Rik van Hulst is director of the Schouwburg in Arnhem.
Agnes Joseph is a social anthropologist, researcher aid and trade between East and West Europe and the developing countries.
John Stringham is a consultant and facilitator.
Geke van der Wal is a free lance journalist, for among others, *de Volkskrant*.

116

Participants of the workshop «Crossing boundaries: Art policy in a multicultural society»

Marco Bentz van de Berg, the Netherlands, Secretary General of the Amsterdam Arts Council.

Peter Blackman, Great Britain, head of the Department of Cultural Diversity of the Arts Council of Great Britain.

Eltje Bos, the Netherlands, head of the Department of Extramural Arts Education and Amateur Arts of the Dutch Ministry of Culture.

Liesbeth van Droffelaar, the Netherlands, staff member of the Policy Division of the Department of Culture of the Utrecht City Council.

Rudi Kross, Surinam/the Netherlands, writer, publicist and television editor, member of the Dutch Arts Council.

Alle de Jonge, the Netherlands, director of the Rotterdam Arts Council, chairman of Witte de With, Center for Contemporary Art in Rotterdam.

Atzo Nicolai, the Netherlands, Secretary General of the Dutch Arts Council.

Henk Scholten, the Netherlands, director of the National Performing Arts Fund.

John Schuster, Surinam/the Netherlands, researcher at the Department of Cultural Anthropology, Utrecht University, and member of the Amsterdam Arts Council.

Driss EL Yazami, Algeria/France, works as an independent journalist and is director of Génériques, an organisation specialised in the history and culture of migrants in France.

Participants of the workshop «Wider landscapes: Defining quality in the arts»

Paolo Bianchi, Italy/Switzerland, cultural critic, publicist and curator.

Chris Dercon, Belgium, director of Witte de With, Center for Contemporary Art, in Rotterdam.

Erica Kubic, the Netherlands, art historian.

John Leerdam, Curaçao/the Netherlands, theater and film director, member of the Artistic Board of Cosmic Illusion.

Sarat Maharaj, South Africa/Great Britain, lectures in Art History and Theory at Goldsmiths College, University of London.

Adi Martis, Aruba/the Netherlands, art historian, currently researching and teaching at the University of Utrecht.

Sevil Özsariyildiz, Turkey/the Netherlands, lecturer, architect, and head of a research team at the Faculty of Architecture of the Technical University of Delft.

Leonie See, Germany, studied Theatre Science, Art History and German Language.

Zafer Senocak, Turkey/Germany, has lived in Germany since 1970 and studied German Language, Politics and Philosophy in Munich. Since 1979 he has published poems and essays in German.

Karim Traïdia, Algeria/the Netherlands, a film director working in the Netherlands.

Mirjam Westen, the Netherlands, art historian and curator for the Gemeentemuseum Arnhem in the Netherlands.

Participants of the workshop «New connections: Finding tomorrow's audience today»

Manus Brinkman, the Netherlands, director of the Association of Museums in the Netherlands.

June Givanni, Great Britain, African & Caribbean Film Officer at the British Film Institute.

Remo Guidieri, co-founder of the Laboratoire d'ethnologie et de sociologie comparative of the University of Paris X, Nanterre. Guidieri is also co-founder and co-editor of *RES*, and Distinguished Visiting Professor at the Cooper Union, School of Architecture, in New York.

Winston Kout, Surinam/the Netherlands, director of Coloured Holland, an employment agency for migrants.

Nora Roozemond, the Netherlands, inspector for drama, dance and literature education for the Ministry of Health, Welfare and Cultural Affairs, focusing on extramural arts education and amateur arts.

Huib Schippers, the Netherlands, musician (Indian sitar), head of the World Music Department of the Music School in Amsterdam and Coordinator of World Music for the Association of Educational Institutes for Music and the Arts in the Netherlands.

Cas Smithuijsen, the Netherlands, director of the Boekman Foundation for research on art- and cultural policy.

Walter Tjon, Surinam/the Netherlands, director of the Scarabes Foundation (migrant arts advisors).

Oscar Wibaut, the Netherlands, deputy director of the Koninklijke Schouwburg in The Hague.

CIP-DATA KONINKLIJKE BIBLIOTHEEK,
THE HAGUE

Cultural

Cultural diversity in the arts : Art, art policies
and the facelift of Europe / ed. by Ria Lavrijsen ;
[transl. Karen Gamester]. – Amsterdam : Royal
Tropical Institute
With bibliogr.
ISBN 90-6832-244-3
NUGI 651
Subject headings: art ; Europe / art policy ;
Europe / cultural policy; Europe

Translation: Karen Gamester – Amsterdam
Cover: Nel Punt – Amsterdam
Printing: Veenman Drukkers, Wageningen
ISBN 90 6832 244 3
NUGI 651